LOSS AND WONDER AT
THE WORLD'S END

Loss and Wonder at the World's End

LAURA A. OGDEN

DUKE UNIVERSITY PRESS   Durham and London   2021

© 2021 Duke University Press
All rights reserved
Printed in the United States of America on acid-free paper ∞
Project Editor: Lisl Hampton
Cover designed by Matthew Tauch
Text designed by Aimee C. Harrison
Typeset in Portrait Text and Univers LT Std by
Tseng Information Systems, Inc.

Library of Congress Cataloging-in-Publication Data
Names: Ogden, Laura, [date] author.
Title: Loss and wonder at the world's end / Laura A. Ogden.
Description: Durham : Duke University Press, 2021. |
Includes bibliographical references and index.
Identifiers: LCCN 2021001838 (print)
LCCN 2021001839 (ebook)
ISBN 9781478013631 (hardcover)
ISBN 9781478014560 (paperback)
ISBN 9781478021865 (ebook)
Subjects: LCSH: Environmental degradation—Great Island
(Argentina and Chile) | Human ecology—Great Island (Argentina
and Chile) | Imperialism. | Great Island (Argentina and Chile)—
Environmental conditions—21st century. | BISAC: SOCIAL
SCIENCE Anthropology Cultural & Social | HISTORY Latin
America South America
Classification: LCC GE160.A7 O34 2021 (print) | LCC GE160.A7 (ebook) |
DDC 333.70982/76—dc23
LC record available at https://lccn.loc.gov/2021001838
LC ebook record available at https://lccn.loc.gov/2021001839

Cover art: Photograph by Charles Wellington Furlong, 1907.
MSS-197, Box XXIV, Folder 6, Furlong Papers, Rauner Special
Collections Library, Dartmouth College.

For Pat and Eva Kelly

Contents

THE WORLD'S END · A FIGURE · 1

Introduction · **Loss and Wonder** · 4

THE EXPLORER'S REFRAIN · A FIGURE · 15

Chapter One · **The Earth as Archive** · 21

ARTURO ESCOBAR · A FIGURE · 44

THE ARCHIVAL EARTH · A FIGURE · 47

Chapter Two · **Alternative Archives of the Present** · 51

LICHENS ON THE BEACH · A FIGURE · 57

Chapter Three · **An Empire of Skin** · 62

THE ANTHROPOLOGIST · A FIGURE · 86

Chapter Four · **Stolen Images** · 91

LEWIS HENRY MORGAN · A FIGURE · 107

Chapter Five · **Dreamworlds of Beavers** · 111

TRACES OF DERRIDA · A FIGURE · 127

ANNE CHAPMAN · A FIGURE · 130

Conclusion · **Birdsong** · 133

GRATITUDE · A FIGURATION · 141

NOTES · 145 — BIBLIOGRAPHY · 169 — INDEX · 183

The World's End · *A Figure*

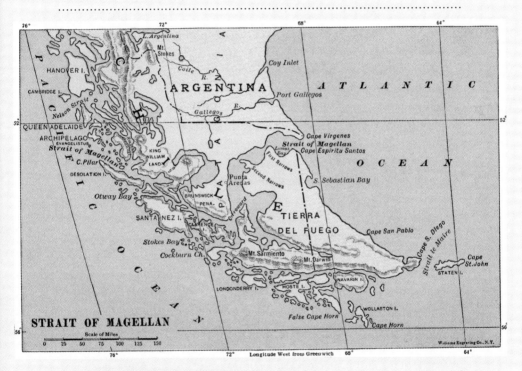

FI.I Map of the Fuegian Archipelago, including the islands of Tierra del Fuego and Cape Horn. By James Bryce, 1st Viscount Bryce, 1838–1922.

The islands of the Fuegian Archipelago are fragments of land, broken off from South America's continental tip. They remind me of the way the jutting bits of family heirlooms are always vulnerable to neglectful care: teacup handles, the outstretched arm of a porcelain ballerina. But when you are on the islands, it is clear that there will be no putting things back together. Instead, the islands of Tierra del Fuego and Cape Horn seem to be barely holding their ground against the rough marriage of the Pacific and Atlantic Oceans. Here, particularly around Cape Horn, so close to the Antarctic Peninsula, enormous tanker ships are dwarfed and battered by tremendous walls of water. These are seas that make worlds and take them too.

Generations of slow-moving glaciers created the archipelago's topographic features, which Charles Wellington Furlong, a central figure in this book, described as "an inconceivable labyrinth of tortuous, storm-swept waterways."[1] These windswept islands are in a constant state of change. Once, the Strait of Magellan was solid ice. Later, during the Little Ice Age, numerous icebergs clogged the channel, endangering the passage of Spanish merchant ships. Today ice-blue glaciers reach down from the high peaks of the southern Andes into these waterways.[2]

The archipelago's naming conventions are not straightforward. For example, many contemporary writers use *Tierra del Fuego* to refer to the entire archipelago. For locals, and within the historic literature, that name refers to the archipelago's largest island, though sometimes you hear *Isla Grande*, which reflects the island's current name.[3] In historic accounts, including archival sources used in this book, the region may be referred to as *Fuegia* and its Indigenous peoples *Fuegians*. There are many more variations of these names, all of which are complicated by different practices in Argentina and Chile. For example, Indigenous people native to the interior of Tierra del Fuego (the big island) are called *Selk'nam* by Chileans and *Ona* by Argentines. In Chile, *Yagán* is generally preferred by the coastal community itself, though you also see *Yaghan* and *Yahgan* as spelling variants. In Argentina, *Yamana* was more common, particularly in ethnographic accounts.

While the names of people and places are varied, describing this region as "the World's End" is fairly ubiquitous. There are World's End backpacker lodges, poem anthologies, cruise ship itineraries, and nature reserves. Travel writers cannot resist the term. As I have explored in my writing about the Florida Everglades, figures are repetitive tropes, phrases, images, or ideas that shape our encounters with the world.[4] Figures emerge out of a specific "apparatus," such as colonialism or capitalism.[5] Figures limit the possible trajectories of life's constellations. For example, the figure of the "worthless swamp" enabled widespread drainage and development in the Florida Everglades in the late nineteenth century. As the Everglades example illustrates, figures are one of the ways territory, both material and semiotic, is claimed.

In many ways, the World's End is the most recognizable figure in the Fuegian Archipelago. It is as common in the serious literature as it is in popular culture. For example, the most widely read book about the region is E. Lucas Bridges's *Uttermost Part of the Earth*, published in 1948. Dog-eared copies of *Uttermost* can be found in the common rooms of nearly every hostel in southern Patagonia, perhaps superseded in popularity only by Bruce Chatwin's *In Patagonia*. In *Uttermost*, Bridges offers an exhaustive chronicle of his family's missionary efforts, settlement, and relations with Fuegian Selk'nam and Yagán families. The book opens with the family's arrival in 1871. After an arduous sea crossing from England, Bridges's weakened and exhausted mother gazes off the schooner's bow toward the shore and recalls her husband's description of their new home: "He had told her of the unkind climate, of the long, dreary winter nights, of the solitude, when one was completely cut off from the outside world, with league after league of impassible country separating one from the nearest settlement of civilized man. . . . In this wild and desolate region, he had told her, there were neither doctors nor police nor government of any kind; and, instead of kindly neighbours, one was surrounded by, and utterly at the mercy of, lawless tribes without discipline or religion."[6] As Bridges's passage illustrates, the World's End figure conveys a sense of extremity that exceeds its geography. While the World's End does suggest a kind of dangerous landscape (as in, *these islands could slide right off the map*), it is a figure that also suggests an unsavory moral terrain, a geography that lies beyond "civilization": *no doctors, no religion, no laws*. Though the imperial politics of the World's End is not subtle, it is also strikingly persistent.[7]

In the Fuegian Archipelago, the World's End is almost elemental, like a life force. The apocalyptic tenor of the World's End resonates with the ways we understand the present as a time of ecological precarity and the way the future is imagined. In this book, the World's End does double duty: it helps me explore the atmospherics of risk associated with the archipelago's emplacement in history, as well as the temporal dimensions of living in times of loss and wonder.

INTRODUCTION · Loss and Wonder

1.1 Glaciers in the Strait of Magellan, Fuegian Archipelago, 1908. Photograph by Charles Wellington Furlong.

The future is dark, with a darkness as much of the womb
as the grave.—REBECCA SOLNIT, *Hope in the Dark*

LIVING IN TIMES OF LOSS

Loss seems to define our present era, particularly losses associated with climate and other forms of environmental change. Best-selling books, from Elizabeth Kolbert's *The Sixth Extinction: An Unnatural History* to Amitav Ghosh's *The Great Derangement: Climate Change and the Unthinkable*, frame the present as a moment in world history where catastrophic losses exceed our imaginative capacities. Each day, it seems, we learn about another species lost to extinction, or a coastline threatened by rising seas. In 2018 the *New York Times Magazine* featured a story titled "Losing Earth: The Decade We Almost Stopped Climate Change." In it, Nathaniel Rich cataloged the opportunities we missed to change the course of the earth's history. Because we did not act, Rich says, "long-term disaster is now the best-case scenario."

When I began to write this book, a crack in Larsen C, one of Antarctica's largest ice shelves, kept me awake at night. My dreams were troubled by fears of a continent broken in half. A few months later, my days and nights became vigils of waiting for the worst—as Hurricane Irma made its way across the warm Caribbean seas toward my childhood home in southern Florida. Loss makes it hard to keep things in perspective.

My family survived Hurricane Andrew, a category 5 storm on the Saffir-Simpson Scale, which made landfall in southern Florida in 1992. The storm's lethal eye crossed over our historic house, built in the 1920s of local pine boards and metal shingles. The day after the storm, I drove down from Gainesville, where I was in graduate school, to our small town at the edge of Everglades National Park. When I reached our town, the landscape had been so altered, with every palm tree, street sign, and building torn apart, that I had to ask the National Guard to help me find my way.

In Roland Barthes's memoir of his mother's death, he describes the landscape of loss as a "flat, dreary country—virtually without water—and paltry."[1] These days, loss doesn't seem like a dry and empty desert. Instead, loss is soggy, a terrain of wet clothes and sodden drywall. Loss is a place where trees and washing machines and playhouses are swept away by the tides. Loss is a way of being in the world marked by grief, rage, fear, and anxiety. Loss transforms who we are, how we relate to other beings and things, and our hopes for the future.

Loss also has its ripple effects. With Larsen C's protective buffer gone, glaciers behind it will begin to melt and break apart. Already communities from the Bering Sea to coastal Louisiana are in the process of relocating their ancestral homes to higher and safer ground. Not long ago, residents of Innaarsuit fled as an 11-million-ton glacier threatened their coastal village in western Greenland.[2] As communities pack up and leave, they sacrifice much more than houses, schools, shops, and livelihoods. For place-based people, the sea is forcefully claiming their past, their sacred sites, and the resting places of their kin, both human and nonhuman.

Loss is not just an event of absence—of something or someone now gone. Instead, loss is ongoing. It is a disposition of alarm and resignation. In this time of loss, everything feels like it needs to be fortified or reengineered. Cities throughout the world have created sustainability plans focused on an uncertain future. In southern Florida, tidal floods now turn city streets into rivers of urban debris. My sister-in-law's car was totaled after she stalled out in a flooded parking lot. People complain that homeowners insurance is hard to find and too expensive anyway. There, contemporary wisdom includes "Sell while you still can" and "Time to get the hell out of Dodge."

Loss is a refrain of the present. Much of the discussion about climate change and rates of species extinctions presents these phenomena as global and therefore universally distributed in space and time. It is as if the earth, once a glimmering blue marble in space, has now become shrouded by a dark and menacing cloud. Seeing the earth and our future as uniform is a trick of scalar perspective, as Anna Tsing has described, which makes us "ignore (not see) the heterogeneity of the world."[3] Instead, loss is expressed in diverse dialects and includes profound silences. Loss and change in southern Florida is not the same as loss and change in the Arctic. Loss has its own vernaculars and place-based temporalities, even though these differences are often effaced by modernity's monocular optics.[4]

Loss is lived by bodies that exist in relation to other beings and things. Loss can rupture or reconfigure those relations. Thom van Dooren reminds us that understanding the full story of loss, such as the ongoing effects of species extinctions, requires "an attentiveness to entanglements."[5] This means paying attention to how loss becomes habituated in the bodies of historically constituted subjects, both human and nonhuman, and how loss saturates the webs of relations that make life. This kind of attentiveness to loss's dialects, affects, and embodiments requires paying attention to the routines and relations of living, dying, and recomposing for the future. As an anthropologist, I understand that time is not a universal phenomenon and that losses are rarely equally distributed. This book offers an account of loss specific to time and place, what could be called *a vernacular of loss*.

Like all places in the world, the Fuegian Archipelago is both real and imagined. The dominant imagined version, what I call the World's End, has long relied on ideas of sublime nature and "lost" peoples to maintain itself. Today the Fuegian Archipelago (as both a real and an imagined place) is being transformed by other concerns about loss. Repeated algal blooms have closed fisheries in the archipelago, collapsing one of the only sources of livelihood for coastal communities. Extractive industries, including commercial forestry and natural gas production, salmon farming, and introduced species, are rapidly transforming constellations of life. Glaciers are in retreat. These are very real and devastating problems. They are also problems that are deeply entangled with histories of colonialism, an aspect of environmental loss that remains fairly invisible in the region.

WONDER

Wonder is another refrain that runs through this book.

Numerous scholars have explored the changing meaning of the term *wonder*, from philosophers to theologians.[6] Since I am neither, I will only say that wonder carries some intellectual baggage. From the Renaissance to the Victorian era, European and Euro-American explorers and naturalists experienced wonder as a kind of spiritual-epistemological disposition toward unfamiliar landscapes and ways of life. Because nature, in its grandest and most exotic variants, offered evidence of a Christian god's earthly miracles, wonder-seekers were motivated by the promise of transcendence, even as they were driven to acquire, dominate, and categorize the lives and landscapes they encountered.[7] The enduring popularity of *Wunderkammer*, those "curiosity cabinets" filled with skulls, artifacts, rocks, fossils, and other specimens, speaks to this dual impulse to both know and acquire the world.

Wonder, as a kind disposition to know and acquire nature, inspired numerous explorers to come to the Fuegian Archipelago, as the anthropologist Anne Chapman describes in her book *European Encounters with the Yamana People of Cape Horn, before and after Darwin*. Chapman's title draws attention to Darwin's visit to the region in 1832, and for good reason. Darwin's infamous depictions of Fuegians as uncivilized savages has overdetermined how the region and its peoples are represented and known. For this reason, Darwin appears as a key figure in my book (as does Anne Chapman).

Darwin was clearly grappling with the limitations of his own experience, to put it mildly. He marvels over the new species he encountered while in the archipelago, while simultaneously expressing feelings of insignificance in the face of the vast unknown that is nature. Describing Cape Horn, he writes, "No one can stand in these solitudes unmoved, and not feel that there is more in man than the mere breath of his body."[8] For the young naturalist, and countless others who came after him, the Fuegian Archipelago offered a mode of nature resonant with transcendent possibility, while at the same time serving as a living laboratory for thinking about nature's laws and change in species.[9]

Darwin's wonder continues to shape the experience of today's nature-loving visitors. Considered one of the last wilderness areas on earth, Tierra del Fuego and Cape Horn have become bucket-list destinations for adventure travelers. Just a short flight from Antarctica, wealthy tourists often spend a few days in the region before heading down to the pole. While in the archipelago, they might take a tour boat through the Beagle Channel's glacial passages or a ferry across the choppy Strait of Magellan. Birders come to see penguins and pink flamingos. Wonder takes flight with the condors. Climbers and trekkers summit the craggy peaks of the southernmost Andes, while salmon and trout fishermen wade the Fuegian rivers to fly fish for (introduced) king salmon and other trout species. Like Patagonia to the north, the archipelago's ongoing allure rests on its reputation as a refuge of spectacular nature, free from the contaminating influence of civilization. My friend Marcos Mendoza has called this vernacular of wonder the "Patagonian sublime."[10]

Yet the World's End is not free of people. Instead, simplistic stereotypes of Fuegian Indigenous peoples are bound up in the archipelago's wilderness aesthetic, particularly representations of Selk'nam and Yagán families from the early twentieth century.[11] The World's End, as a set of compositional practices, collapses "wild people" into "wild nature." In tourist shops all over Punta Arenas, for example, there are postcards of penguins, glaciers, and Selk'nam people all crammed into the same display rack. Images of the Selk'nam *Hain* ceremony are everywhere: the walls of backpacker hostels, book covers, coffee mugs, tea towels. The *Yagán* is the name of the commercial ferry that makes the thirty-hour trip to Navarino Island, a favorite spot for European trekkers. The ferry's cramped galley is decorated with vintage images of semi-clothed Yagán people. Although Indigenous communities continue to live in the archipelago, these images contribute to the near invisibility of contemporary Indigenous lives and livelihoods in the region.

It doesn't help that these images are almost always captioned with a reference to the "lost tribes" of the World's End. The trope of the lost tribes, with its connotations of extinction, is so pervasive even most Chileans are unaware that Yagán, Selk'nam, and Kawésqar families continue to live in the region.[12]

Of course, the association of nature with Native peoples is by no means unique to the Fuegian Archipelago. As the daughter of 1970s white hippie scientists, I am fairly experienced in the ways Indigeneity has been (and continues to be) appropriated by nature lovers in the United States. In Chile these modes of appropriation are similar. For example, almost all the nature parks in the archipelago evoke the landscape's Indigenous history and the "lost tribes" iconography as part of their branding approach. When I am in these parks, I can't seem to escape earnest people wanting to lecture me about Selk'nam ceremonies or medicinal plant use, all gleaned from anthropology of the early twentieth century.

Yet in these nature-loving sites, something else is going on. Fuegian peoples are not only represented as relics of the past (as they are in tourist shops and on book covers) or even representatives of primeval nature. The "lost people" of the Fuegian Archipelago have come to serve as a warning sign of nature's precarity in this time of ecological crisis. Put another way, evoking lost people has become of way of saying, *If we can lose these nature-people, we can lose this nature too.* Absent is any self-reflection about the "we" (often white nature lovers) in this eco-apocalyptic equation.[13]

But wonder is a shifting refrain, with multiple registers. Wonder can also be a practice of hope shaped by small, ordinary triumphs.[14] This book ar-

I.2 On the left, a figure from the Selk'nam Hain ceremony, the spirit Halahaches, in front of a mobile tourist shop, Punta Arenas, Chile. On the right, Yagán Kina figure painted on the front of a house, Puerto Williams, Chile. Photographs by the author.

chives many forms of loss—including territory, language, sovereignty, and life itself. Yet, as I learned in writing this book, life continues to flourish even in the ruins of these devastations.[15] Coastal lichens hold their ground against the battering tides of rising seas.[16] On Isla Navarino, children learn Yagán vocabulary words in preschool, even when there is only one *abuela* left in the community who grew up speaking the language in her home. I am enormously indebted to the wonder and commitments that drive social movements to seek change, as well as the wonder and commitments that enable guanaco populations to rebound after decades of overhunting on Tierra del Fuego.[17]

If the present is a time of loss, it is also a time when communities (of people and other living beings) are grappling with loss, holding their ground, and becoming something new in the process. The darkness of the womb, as Rebecca Solnit says, is a darkness filled with uncertainty, as well as the possibility of a different future.[18]

COMPOSITIONAL NOTES

Three questions guide this book:

1 What evidence do we use to know the present?
2 Where is this evidence archived?
3 What temporalities constitute the present?

The *place* of this book is the Fuegian Archipelago of southernmost South America. The *time* of this book is the heterogeneous lost-times produced by the ongoing effects of settler colonialism in the region. The *form* of this book is an archive of loss and wonder. That said, my ideas about place, time, and form have become increasingly unsettled in the course of writing this book.

This book's materials draw from both collaborative ethnographic research in the Fuegian Archipelago as well as collaborative archival research at Dartmouth College, where I work. Like many environmental anthropologists, my research has explored how some conservation efforts transform the lives and livelihoods of other communities, as well as the political and economic forces, generally glossed as capitalism, that continue to transform multispecies practices of living and dying throughout the world. I began fieldwork in the region because I wanted to understand more about the politics and ethics of managing animals considered "invasive." Simply,

I wondered: How can it be OK to kill animals just because they are in the wrong place? I went to Tierra del Fuego to find out.

While introduced species are changing landscapes everywhere, beavers imported into the Fuegian Archipelago in 1948 have become one of the most challenging forest conservation problems in the world, as I describe in this book. Spending time with people who care about the Fuegian forests taught me the importance of allowing loss to serve as a generative space for ethnographic theory and environmental ethics. Fuegian beavers taught me to pay attention to the way animal life is enrolled in ongoing imperial projects. Fuegian beavers also taught me a bit about wonder.

While anthropological research tends to benefit from serendipitous encounters, this project shifted significantly through a chance conversation with Alfredo Prieto, a respected Chilean archaeologist. Prieto urged me to explore the archives of an American explorer, Charles Wellington Furlong, which are housed a short walk from my office at Dartmouth College. As it turns out, the Furlong archive contains one of the world's most significant collections of materials that document the impacts of colonial settlement on the lives of Fuegian Indigenous peoples and their landscapes. Trying to make sense of the archive and the college's ethical responsibilities as stewards of this material led to a rich working relationship with members of the Comunidad Indígena Yaghan Bahía Mejillones on Isla Navarino. We have taken a collaborative approach to the archive: Francisco Filgueira and Alberto Serrano have come to Dartmouth to make copies of material and evaluate the archive's scope and importance, and I have led several meetings at Villa Ukika, the Yagán community on Isla Navarino, to discuss the archive's contents and develop practices for making the materials available and useful to the community.

I began the research for this book in 2011, with an interest in learning about the impacts of environmental change on life in the Fuegian Archipelago. Soon after I began spending time in the region, it became clear that the legacies of colonialism, though everywhere, were largely absent from discussions about environmental change. This is striking, as many would agree that the present, at least in the Americas, is the product of various forms of global imperialism. In the process of writing this book, I began to think of environmental change as imperialism's shadow, a darkness cast upon the earth in the wake of other losses.

Sometimes big concepts explain everything and nothing at the same time. This book uses ethnographic research to understand the sites, or "contact zones," to borrow Mary Louise Pratt's term, where environmental change and colonialism touch and compose life in the Fuegian Archipelago.[19] It is the touching that matters. Loss and wonder are produced in these sites of contact, though they are discernible in shifting registers depending on the context and politics of their production. The loss and wonder of colonial explorers and the loss and wonder of contemporary environmentalists are not the same. Loss and wonder are always subjective and political.

As an example: the other morning I was standing in my kitchen making a sandwich. As I stood there, I could just make out the sounds of Elvis Presley coming from my daughter's room on the floor above. I imagined her getting ready for school, music blaring, as she struck a pose in front of the bathroom mirror. The song's melody was muffled, yet Elvis's familiar low voice seeped through the floorboards. With it came sweet and sad memories of watching Elvis movies on a grainy television in my mother's bedroom. He seemed from another age, even then. Yet my Elvis nostalgia is dulled by a dose of Elvis despair, shaped by the ways Elvis's fame ("the King of Rock and Roll") effaced so many Black artists in the history of rock and roll. Loss and wonder are like political currents that creep under the door on a cold day. Sometimes you barely feel them, yet they can still chill you.

This book is organized as an archive of loss and wonder. John Berger has compared archives to archaeological sites, which is apt, except that most archives are curated in ways that archaeological sites are not. Archives are more than a collection of facts, memories, photographs, digital files, and dried leaves pressed flat and brown in the pages of an old book. Archives have structuring logics that constrain how the world is known and how the past is encountered. Archives are sites of both proliferation and restraint. Not everything gets in, only things that matter. It is this "mattering" that we need to pay attention to, as this is a key to understanding an archive's logic.[20]

In this case, I am extending the epistemological boundaries of what counts as evidence in an archive of the present.[21] In this book's archive, I am bringing together beings and things (beavers, stolen photographs, lichen, birdsong, my cousin's pantry) to catalog the ways environmental change and colonial history are entangled. In the process, I have learned that the present is composed of heterogeneous temporalities and that loss and wonder are contingent refrains. That said, my aim is not diagnostic. Instead, I am writing my way in and out of these entanglements.

An experimental approach to wonder, what I call speculative wonder, has guided my research method and thinking. In general, speculative wonder is a curiosity about other assemblages of life (compositions of beings, beings and things, sometimes beings that identify as human), but more specifically, *it is an experimental approach to engaging and representing those worlds.* Bringing an ethnographic sensibility to trajectories of species difference, for example about the lives of beavers, is clearly a speculative project.[22] When speculating about nonhuman worlds, I pay particular attention to how other beings sense and know their environments. It matters that beavers have very poor eyesight. Yet, instead of collapsing these speculations into the "already known" of animal biology or ecology (though these are clearly important sources of knowledge in my work), my speculations are guided by an intentional hyper-anthropomorphism. In other words, I use what I know best (my own subjectivity) to engage the affective worlds of other species. In some ways, this allows me to shift an epistemological and ontological problem (how other beings know the world) to a representational one (how to write these worlds).

Wonder, as the philosopher Isabelle Stengers has explained, "means both to be surprised and entertain questions."[23] Stengers has written about the philosophical challenge of bringing nonhumans into political theory as entities with political standing.[24] She uses the term *speculative* to signal an experimental reframing that enables the ontological reorientation in our practices of environmental concern. For Stengers, life forms are always in the process of becoming, which means the future is one of possibility. The goal of the thought experiment is not to speculate about possible alternative futures but to reveal the tensions that are a part of becoming within the confines of the world's predetermined categories (what she calls "probabilities").[25]

Thought experiments are the nudge that helps us ask, *What if?* Formal thought experiments in my book, such as reframing invasive species as "animal diasporas," allow me to critically evaluate intellectual traditions that tend to keep animals, plants, and humans in separate conceptual spaces. With a similar goal in mind, this book experiments with disciplinary boundaries and genres, bringing together ethnography, colonial archives, performance studies, and natural history. This expansiveness helps me nudge concepts that feel stagnant, like "wilderness" or "invasive species," and, to quote Stengers, produce "narratives that populate our worlds and imaginations in different ways."[26]

Finally, instead of a classic literature review, this book includes several portraits of figures whose ideas have been influential to this book. The accumulation of these portraits, like the World's End that began this book, form the book's intellectual archive. The book includes portraits of well-known philosophers, such as Jacques Derrida, and anthropologists who have been important to my thinking, such as Arturo Escobar and Anne Chapman, other collaborator-friends, as well as other beings and places. I have treated these figures like playing cards inserted between the pages of my book. This approach helps me treat theory as just another form of knowledge, specific to place, time, and social relations, rather than a kind of apolitical, universal knowledge.

While this book explores the vernaculars of loss and wonder in the Fuegian Archipelago, much of the wisdom I have about these emplaced practices comes from my long-term fieldwork in the Florida Everglades. As a writer, I struggled to keep the Everglades out of this book—until I decided that it was impossible. Not only did I write and think about the Everglades for nearly two decades, but I grew up in the Everglades and was raised by Everglades scientists. The Everglades landscape is as foundational to my thinking self as the figures I highlight in the archive's portraits. And so she finds her way in.

The Explorer's Refrain · *A Figure*

F2.1 Charles Wellington Furlong and Virginia Spinney Furlong curating his archive, Dartmouth College, May 1962.

There is an obsessional madness to working in the archives, a point the philosopher Jacques Derrida made in his work *Archive Fever*.[1] I have spent the past several years plundering the collected papers of Colonel Charles Wellington Furlong, an American who traveled in the Fuegian Archipelago in 1907–8, returning again in 1911. For Derrida, the archivist project is fueled by a desperate desire to locate authentic evidence of a knowable past. Not surprisingly, this mad quest has its physical symptoms. After spending hours hunched over document boxes and squinting at bad handwriting, my back has stiffened, and my eyes are strained. The collection takes up thirty-five linear feet in the backroom storage areas of Dartmouth College Library's Rauner Special Collections Library. Most of the time, these materials lie dormant in anonymous gray boxes.

Archival research involves strict protocols: ink pens are not allowed; purses and backpacks must be secured in off-site locations; gum and food are not permitted; sometimes wearing gloves is required. While working in the archive, I took thousands of photographs, but I was always nervous about the use of flash photography. In archives, materials are meticulously cataloged, tracked, and hand-delivered, as if in a police procedural. But the culture of Rauner Library is nothing like a TV detective show. Like most archives, Rauner's ambience of serious scholarship makes me feel like an amateur. I think of Agatha Christie's Miss Marple, impatient with protocols and lacking the professional's commitment to rigor.

After several years in the archive, I have come to know Furlong, or at least his archival self, well. Born in 1874, less than a decade after the US Civil War, Furlong fully embodied the contradictions and blind spots of white, liberal America's ideas about race and Indigenous peoples. As part of the acquisition process, Dartmouth College hired him to organize, catalog, and interpret his collection.[2] Being both archival subject and its sole interpreter allowed Furlong to present a highly curated version of his self, first, as an explorer, and in his later years as a scientist.

Spending time with Furlong has granted me a certain expertise on explorer culture.[3]

Furlong's life of accomplishments was long, varied, and full of many firsts. He discovered the wreck of the US frigate *Philadelphia*; he was a rodeo star; and he created the US Geographic Military Intelligence Division during World War I. He was friends with Teddy Roosevelt and Herbert Hoover. He recovered the relics of Sir Henry M. Stanley while exploring East and Central Africa. Yet in a 1948 letter to Lucas Bridges, one of the founding settlers of Tierra del Fuego, Furlong wrote, "Of all my many and varied explorations in out-of-the-way lands, whether in the hinterlands of Bolivia, the jungles of Surinam, the back Orinoco country of Venezuela, in the Balkan backlands or with my Arab friends of the Sahara, in the deserts of the Middle East, Tripoli and Morocco, with the Masai and the Kikuyu and other tribes of East and Central Africa, *my deepest heart interest* somehow seems still to be in my expeditions in Tierra del Fuego with you, in particular, and the Lawrences and my Ona and Yagan friends."[4] It should be clear from this passage that exploration is a masculine endeavor, forever preoccupied with penetrating the unknown. Sometimes, though, an explorer's memories become bittersweet with age.[5]

Another thing I learned: the distance between "Furlong the Explorer" and "Furlong the Archivist" was not a straightforward march in the direction of liberal progress. In significant ways, the culture of US imperialism changed between Furlong's initial trip to the Fuegian Archipelago in 1907 and when he was curating his archive in the early 1960s. To illustrate, he left for Tierra del Fuego just a few years after the United States signed the Treaty of Paris in 1898, ending the Spanish-American War and solidifying the United States' imperial presence in the Caribbean. During his journey, Furlong actually crossed paths with Theodore Roosevelt's Great White Fleet, the nickname for the US armada that was then circumnavigating the globe as a demonstration of US naval power.

Fast-forward fifty years. When Furlong was working at Dartmouth, the geopolitics of US imperialism and other forms of coloniality were quite different (at least overtly). For example, in 1961, the year after Dartmouth acquired Furlong's collection, Frantz Fanon published *The Wretched of the Earth*, a soaring manifesto that inspired liberation movements for decades to come, including the Black Panthers. That same year, the National Indian Youth Council was formed, one of the first Native American organizations to use direct action to protect treaty rights in the United States. On the Dartmouth campus, students and faculty were engaged in civil rights marches and demonstrations, as the nightly news made the violent attacks on African American protesters in the South difficult to ignore.

And yet, while the formal apparatus of colonialism and empire may have been crumbling in Algeria, Cuba, and Oakland, California, their traces remain throughout the Furlong archive (as they continue to reverberate in sites of neoliberal and territorial occupation in the United States today). For example, on the back of every photograph in the archive, and there are about seven hundred that document life in the Fuegian Archipelago, Furlong affixed a typed and detailed caption. At some point, when reading these cap-

> It was 3 years after this when Furlong succeeded in the second attempt as the first American explorer and second white man to effect an entrance into this terra incognita. This expedition was made with 4 Ona, all known to the Bridges as killers. Bridges' experiences are described in his classic book, "Uttermost Part of the Earth" and Furlong's in a series of feature articles in Harper's Magazines between 1908 and 1912. Furlong considers Lucas Bridges, who died later in 1949, as the greatest authority on the Ona Amerinds. Furlong is the only living authority (1964).
>
> Collection Charles Wellington Furlong

F2.2 A variant of the explorer's refrain from a lengthy caption that describes Furlong's long-term association with E. Lucas Bridges, the first white man to cross the interior of Tierra del Fuego.

tions (which someone told me his wife actually typed), I stopped keeping track of the number of times Furlong referred to himself in the following way: "the first American and second white man to explore the interior of Tierra del Fuego."[6]

Time and time again he used this exact phrase, a refrain of colonial exceptionalism meant to cement his legacy within the archive. Furlong's refrain traveled with him across many continents and several decades before permanently settling here. Reading those captions is like hearing the cover of a song you know well—familiar, yet with slight shifts in the register. Colonial exceptionalism is resilient in that way. Still, the "second" white man? Is this like being the second man on the moon?

Furlong's archival self is unbending with the simplified tropes of white male exploration. Perhaps because of this I yearned to know him as a real person. My genealogical research offered little beyond the vital statistics contained in his marriage and birth certificates. His application to join the Sons of the American Revolution only confirmed what I already knew. Things I wondered about: Why did his first marriage fail? Surely his wife resented his years away. Her name was Eva, also the name of my daughter. Did Furlong miss his children while he was away? Was his missing the same kind of missing that has left me hollow and jagged when I'm doing fieldwork?

Still, I have a strange connection with Furlong forged in the countless hours I have spent with his handwritten journals. I am probably the only person alive who has read them in their entirety.

There is something so confidential and vulnerable about his cramped handwriting, his misspelled words and free-form sentences. His cursive is terrible and contains the traces of prior centuries. For example, his *xs* look

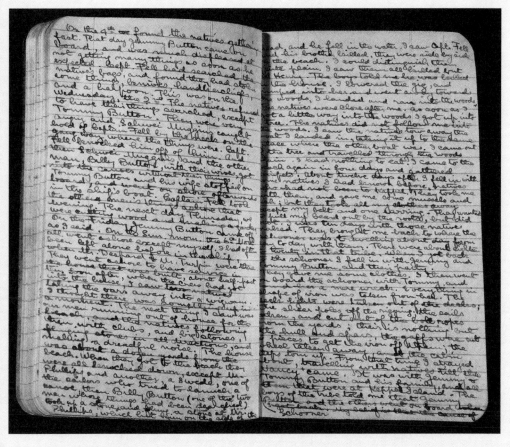

F2.3 An example of Furlong's journals. Photograph by the author.

like crooked *c*s. I had to consult a handbook on old-fashioned writing just to make sense of his letters. I often found myself staring for long minutes at the simplest words, such as *then* or *cape* or even *is*. On nearly every page, and I transcribed 122 single-spaced pages, there are words or passages that I bracketed to mark my uncertainty. A sentence's meaning changes dramatically if a word is *horse* or *house*. Because Furlong was interested in the region's Indigenous peoples, his diaries include endless lists of Selk'nam and Yagán words and names. I found these impossible to decipher. I simply could not figure out the letters when he wasn't writing in English or Spanish. There is an anticipatory logic to transcription, making transcription a form of translation.

Michael Taussig described a fieldwork notebook as "an extension of oneself, if not more self than oneself, like an entirely new organ alongside one's heart and brain, to name the more evocative organs of our inner self."[7] If this is so, Furlong's self is disordered. His journals are a collage of observations and random facts. He bounces from topic to topic, like a stone skipping across the surface of a lake. Some topics are brief, just a couple of words; others take up pages. Some pages are filled with lists of expenses and little reminders to himself. Throughout there are pencil illustrations (boat profiles, rigging, spears, "wigwams"), the lines no longer crisp.

While my own field notes veer off-course, they generally adhere to chronological order. Furlong rarely bothered with dates or the diarist's convention of describing the events of the day, though certain passages do have a feeling of immediacy. For example, in the early days of his trip across the interior of Tierra del Fuego, he describes how the horses slide and stumble down a rocky embankment, only to bog down in the mud at the other side. The animals are so stuck, Furlong fears he will have to abandon Joe, his cargo mule. This passage must have been written before Furlong had a chance to cool down, as his frustration is etched into the page.

Clues allow me to trace some of his movements across the landscape, even though they feel outside of time. For example, his journals include the names of places (lakes, ranches, rivers, coves, etc.) and their descriptions. Because the journals are numbered, I can somewhat follow his route. Many of the places he describes are places I too have visited. I have literally followed in his footsteps. When this happens, his time and space become entangled with my own.

In all my labored time with Furlong, he mentioned his family only once. At the end of February 1908, after nearly a year exploring the Fuegian Archipelago, he and his guide found themselves at a Tehuelche horse camp. The atmosphere in the camp was rough with fighting and liquor, only to worsen after some Argentine rustlers showed up. Furlong became increasingly worried about his safety. His troop of horses mysteriously disappeared during the night. The rustlers were keen on getting his Winchester rifle and his chocolate. That night his handwriting spiraled down the page, becoming large and loopy and faint. He wrote, "I am writing this by sense of touch only. If anything further occurs and there is opportunity I will write it. My thoughts at such a time naturally turn to my darling wife and precious little Ruth and to other loved ones at home. I lay on watching until the crescent of the waning moon kissed the dawn."[8] I am generally a fast reader, but my eyes traveled through his journals slowly and painfully. These journals created vast horizons of lost time, like the time I spend sleeping.

1 · THE EARTH AS ARCHIVE

1.1
Puppup, who served as one of Furlong's guides, stands gazing at the horizon. Interpreting the image, Furlong said, "It represents the last of his fast disappearing tribe looking toward the sunset of their day." Furlong's footprints can be seen in the sand in the bottom right corner.

TRACES OF EXISTENCE

The Furlong Papers collection is enormous and daunting. I did not know where to begin or even how to begin to work on it. So I read over the collection's comprehensive catalog, the "finding aid." In archives, the finding aid indexes a collection's contents, box by box, as well as the contents of each box. For example, the first box contains all of Furlong's collected correspondence. In looking over the finding aid, I noticed one box in the collection containing something called "dermatoglyphs." As I had never seen this word before, I began there.

What I found: manila folder after manila folder, containing the foot- and handprints of Yagán and Selk'nam men, women, and children. In all, the collection contains forty-three hand- and footprints of Fuegian people, as well as impressions of Furlong's and his son's hands and feet, used for ethnological comparison. Most have handwritten descriptions of the subject, with Furlong's soft cursive archiving a different inscription practice.

Furlong does not say much in his journals about the process of taking hand- and footprints, though he published an account of the process in 1966.[1] In his journals, he says Selk'nam living at Harberton, Bridges's estancia on the Beagle Channel, initially were not eager to cooperate with the printing process. Yet after Furlong demonstrated the process, using his

1.2   Footprints of Aanikin (*left*), one of Furlong's guides, and Warkeeo (*right*), one of Aanikin's wives.

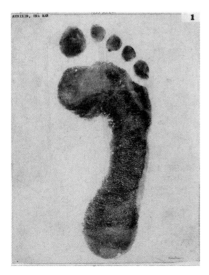 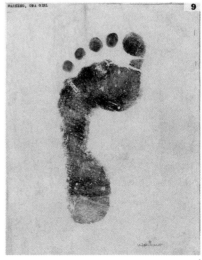

own feet, they "not only were willing, but they were anxious, to help make dermatoglyphs of their own foot and handprints."[2] While camped at Lago Fagnano on his trek across Tierra del Fuego, Furlong made prints of his guide Aanikin's hands and feet.[3] In the field, Furlong used the bottom of a frying pan as the printing surface. The frying pan is supposed to be archived in the Furlong Papers, though I have never seen it.[4]

In general, Furlong's anthropological interests were influenced by nineteenth-century theories that assumed cultural and social difference was an outcome of biological processes, including evolution.[5] The study of hand-, foot-, and fingerprints was part of a larger repertoire of nineteenth-century scientific practices aimed at classifying racial difference using biophysical metrics, such as phrenology or craniometry. Throughout his trip, Furlong measured the height and skull size of Selk'nam and Yagán women, men, and children. One afternoon, he carefully recorded how far Yagán men could throw spears.

Francis Galton, a eugenics pioneer and Darwin's cousin, wrote the definitive account of fingerprint analysis in 1892. In it, we learn that Sir William Herschel introduced the widespread use of fingerprints on contracts and real estate and welfare transactions in colonial India. Herschel developed the protocol out of necessity, Galton explains, since the signatures of Bengali laborers could be easily faked and, moreover, colonial administrators had a very difficult time distinguishing one "native" from another.[6] As the body's signature, fingerprints became evidence of existence, useful in the colonial control and surveillance of bodies.

Galton was a firm believer in the importance of fingerprint analysis to anthropology and science. It had the potential, he wrote, "to throw welcome light on some of the most interesting biological questions of the day."[7] He wrote, "Let no one despise the ridges on account of their smallness, for they are in some respects the most important of all anthropological data."[8] For Galton, the persistence and individuality of fingerprint "minutiae," such as distinct whorls and ridges, made the prints reliable, even after death.[9] His belief that the fragment (fingerprint minutia) could speak for the whole (identity, race, history) parallels the logic of the archive.[10] In the archive, a tattered slip of paper can revise history.

Furlong refers to dermatoglyphs as a "technique of existence."[11] Literally, the term means "skin carving," though the translation should be "traces of existence." Someone or something once existed, and though they are gone, they leave their traces. Several years ago, some months after my mother died, I accidentally erased a message she had left on my answering machine. I remember pushing that button as her voice disappeared. This is how ephemeral traces of existence can be.

Paleontologists use the term *trace fossil* to describe a form of evidence that signals the past presence of biological life while not actually being a fossil itself.[12] Examples of trace fossils include a dinosaur's trackway and the borings and burrows of prehistoric beings upon the earth. The most famous trace fossils are the Laetoli footprints in Tanzania, first discovered by Mary Leakey and her team in 1976. Leakey thought these footprints revealed evidence of the earliest bipedal humans, their journey across the landscape captured in damp volcanic ash which then quickly dried into something akin to cement. The discovery of these footprints touched something profound in Leakey's imagination. She described them as "a kind of poignant time wrench." The Laetoli footprints allowed her to imagine the humanity of our remote ancestors in ways that seemed to transcend time.[13]

The Laetoli beds are an entry in the archival earth, what Leakey called "Nature's ashen ledger."[14] They remind us that all archives, even the earth, are composed of traces of existence. As traces, dermatoglyphs operate in ways that are similar to trace fossils. They register absence and presence simultaneously.

TRACKS AND TRACES

A month after discovering the Furlong dermatoglyphs, I shared them with members of the Yagán community living in Villa Ukika on Isla Navarino. My trip to Navarino had been planned for many months. I was working with my research collaborators Christy Gast and Camila Marambio on a short film about lichen at the Omora Biosphere Reserve, also on Isla Navarino (see "Lichens on the Beach: A Figure"). In the months leading up to this trip, between teaching and other obligations, I managed to grab a few days to look over the Furlong Papers and put together a slide presentation of the photographs and other materials to share with the community. In addition to sharing the collection's contents, I wanted to discuss strategies to make the materials available and Dartmouth's responsibilities to protect potentially sensitive material. For example, Furlong describes some of the sound recordings as containing "songs for the dead," not to mention these recordings are of family members who died decades ago. Peter Carini, college archivist at Dartmouth, shared these concerns and asked for additional guidance from the community about appropriate use and access.

On the first day of our community meeting, I projected hundreds of

1.3 Furlong taking a foot impression of a little girl, with her mother looking on, at the Rio Douglas settlement, 1907. Photograph taken by Rev. John Williams, using Furlong's camera.

images on the wall of the meeting house. Looking through the images was an exceedingly slow process, as we often magnified the photographs section by section. This way, community members could inspect the faces of possible relatives. The small details of daily living—types of clothing, cooking pots, shelters, and even the dogs—were of great interest.

On my walk over to Ukika that morning, I was anxious about showing the dermatoglyphs. I worried that their clinical racism would be painful and, in all honesty, what possessing them said about me. Before projecting the slides of the dermatoglyphs, I explained what they were and cautioned that they might be upsetting. As we looked at them projected on the wall, I was surprised that no one really seemed to care about them, or at least no one said anything. Instead, everyone just wanted to talk about the photographs.

All forms of existence leave their traces. Derrida warns that we should not be lulled into thinking that traces provide access to a fixed past or origin. In contrast to the term's etymology, which includes the idea of a footprint, Derrida did not conceive of the trace as a kind of clue or evidence, like the way a footprint functions in an Agatha Christie novel.[15] In her introduction to Derrida's *Of Grammatology*, Judith Butler helps us understand the unsettling nature of the trace (its play, in Derridean terms): "We expect that where this is a trace, there is something prior to it that has left it—the trace of life, a book, a thought. But if the trace is the means through which what is prior is marked, then it is at once lost and found in the course of that marking."[16]

Not all tracks are traces in the Derridean sense. Hunters I worked with in the Florida Everglades taught me that there is a reliable predictability in certain traces. There is correspondence, for example, between a track and the presence of an animal in space and time. Everglades hunters could read alligator drag marks and tell how many hours had passed since the reptile had lumbered past. According to Furlong, his Selk'nam guides were also amazing trackers. They could follow footprints through moist moss and distinguish one person's prints from another's. An uncle of one of Furlong's guides walked mainly on his toes; his tracks were little more than toe prints.[17] While Galton was unsure about the utility of dermatoglyphs for characterizing race, Selk'nam hunters could distinguish the footprints of a white person from that of a Selk'nam. This practical knowledge, in one instance, prevented a Selk'nam man from being falsely accused of murder.[18]

While the predictability of tracks and other forms of evidence is comforting, not all traces work this way. Some slip from our grasp, just at the moment we are making sense of history and ourselves in the process. Dermatoglyphs are much closer to Derridean traces than clues in a detective story, even though they feel like evidence in a crime scene. Derrida presents us with a contradiction, describing the trace as the absence of presence. It is exactly this ambiguity that is so unsettling about the Furlong dermatoglyphs. The dermatoglyphs offer traces of being in the world, what we might understand as presence, yet simultaneously mark loss.

Almost one year after visiting Villa Ukika, Francisco Filgueira, a Yagán community member, and Alberto Serrano, the director of the Martin Gusinde Anthropological Museum on Isla Navarino, came to Dartmouth to work in the collection with me. During a two-week period we tried to photograph every single item related to Furlong's time in the Fuegian Archipelago. This was an exhausting task, resulting in thousands of high-resolution images. Most of the time we joked like jaded doctors in a triage unit as we barreled through what felt like an endless catalog of loss (of people, languages, ways of being in the world).

Our easy banter stopped when we found an imprint of a little baby's

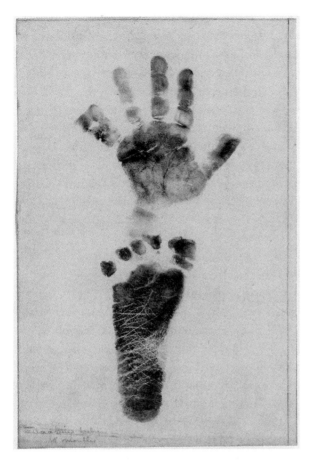

1.4
Prints from Aanikin's four-month-old daughter, taken at Lago Fagnano, January 1908. Seeing these, I could not help but think of the prints I received at the hospital when my daughter was born.

hand and foot. With its protective manila folder lying open on the table, I remember Francisco holding the print in his hands and looking at us. At that moment, Alberto and I leaned in closer to him, the way people who are not friends but becoming friends touch but do not touch. I am not trying to describe melodrama. Instead, just a flutter of sorrow that left us momentarily quiet.

In this moment I learned that traces work in ways that are much more complicated than Derrida considered. True, traces, like the dermatoglyphs, are copies or representations that evoke a real (what Derrida called) presence that is always in the process of dissolving. Yet these dermatoglyphs also carry the past and being-in-the-world forcibly into the present. In doing so, they touch us.

The dermatoglyphs' ability to touch us, or their affective resonance, is bound up in their material presence as artifacts. Their copies (such as the images in this book) do not have the same force of encounter. Kathleen Stewart has described affective encounters as "a kind of contact zone" where "flows of power literally take place."[19] Over a century ago, at a windswept missionary's outpost in the southernmost village in the world, Furlong pressed ink-stained hands and feet onto sheets of clean white paper. In those moments of intimate contact, skin cells mixing with ink, the card stock became infused with traces of another. The dermatoglyphs drag us into the flow of history, a tidal wave of loss, in ways their copies do not. Perhaps this is why people were less interested in the dermatoglyphs when I projected their images on the wall of the Yagán community center.

ANNE CHAPMAN'S RAGE

Traces of existence have many registers, including rage.

The anthropologist Anne Chapman saved her rage for Charles Darwin. Darwin visited the Fuegian Archipelago in 1832, while serving as the naturalist on the voyage of HMS *Beagle*. On Darwin's journey three young Fuegian captives were also on the ship. This is a famous story, told so often that these Fuegians (captured, returned, and made famous) have come to stand in for all Fuegians in the archipelago. To summarize: On HMS *Beagle*'s earlier voyage, in 1830, Captain Robert FitzRoy took four young captives to England, with the intention of introducing them to British customs and society, including King William IV and Queen Adelaide. FitzRoy's crew named these young people Jemmy Button, Fuegia Basket, and York Minster. Fuegia Basket and Jemmy Button were only children. A fourth Yagán captive, who was named Boat Memory, died of smallpox while in England.[20]

Darwin's portrait of the Fuegian captives incited Chapman's rage. For centuries, his descriptions of these Fuegians as savage, less than human, and *the wildest people on earth* profoundly shaped European encounters with Indigenous people in the region. These depictions, inscribed in Darwin's letters and in his published account of the *Beagle*'s journey, continue to circulate and compose the World's End as a figure. I do not feel the need to repeat those stories here.[21] Most of my colleagues who are natural scientists, even if they know nothing about Tierra del Fuego, recall Darwin's descriptions of half-naked Fuegians crowded around fires on the beach. Sir Baldwin Spencer, the Australian anthropologist, visited the region in February 1929, intent on studying "Darwin's Tierra del Fuego."[22] Today Darwin's association with the archipelago has become a way of marking the region's

1.5 Students participating in a course titled Following in Darwin's Footsteps. Beyond the students are the Beagle Channel and the Darwin range. Photograph by the author.

scientific importance. Suffice it to say, these representations continue to define how Yagán people are known today. And it is very painful.

Chapman's rage was a searing eclipse that prevented her from seeing Darwin in any other light. Darwin was only twenty-three years old when he arrived in Tierra del Fuego on the *Beagle*—a mere glimmer of the scholar who would become the author of *On the Origin of Species* (1859). When he began his trip, he was a smart, recent Cambridge graduate, avidly interested in natural history and specimen collection. His view of the world was shaped by his self-described orthodox religious beliefs and his wealthy, albeit progressive, British childhood. In old age, Darwin described his time on the *Beagle* as the most significant event in his life, an experience that determined the trajectory of his entire career.[23] A random detail reveals much about his world at the time of his voyage: When Darwin met Captain FitzRoy, his future boss and five-year cabinmate, the captain nearly rejected Darwin's application to serve as the ship's naturalist. FitzRoy, a committed phrenologist, did not like the shape of Darwin's nose, thinking it revealed a lazy character.[24]

Darwin's Fuegia was no terra incognita. Rather, it was a landscape already fashioned by histories of loss and wonder. To illustrate, in his journals

Darwin recalled the unexpected January storm that trapped the naturalists of HMS *Endeavor* in 1769, killing two in their party, as they, like Darwin, were exploring Fuegia's alpine habitats. But more vividly, the *Beagle*'s entire journey was burdened by its own history in the region. During the ship's first voyage, in 1828, Captain Pringle Stokes, FitzRoy's predecessor, became deeply depressed and inconsolable during navigation of the archipelago's dangerous channels, so much so that he died from complications of a self-inflicted gunshot wound (gangrene) while anchored in the Strait of Magellan.

These tragic histories seem to saturate Darwin's Fuegian experience, lending a kind of World's End atmospherics to his description of the landscape: "There was a degree of mysterious grandeur in mountain behind mountain, with the deep intervening valleys, all covered by one thick, dusky mass of forest. The atmosphere, likewise, in this climate, where gale succeeds gale, with rain, hail, and sleet, seems blacker than anywhere else. In the Strait of Magellan looking due southward from Port Famine, the distant channels between the mountains appeared from their gloominess to lead beyond the confines of this world."[25]

Darwin spent over two months there—for him, a landscape of unpredictable weather, extreme seas, and people he was ill-equipped to understand. Still, while in the archipelago, he crawled through the thick Fuegian forests, scrambled down waterfalls, followed guanaco trails along the coast, and collected forty-nine bird specimens, among other things, while keeping prodigious notes of his explorations.[26]

Darwin, the young and emergent scientist of the HMS *Beagle*, was really not the object of Chapman's rage. Instead she was concerned with Darwin as a figure. As a figure, Darwin is a force that continues to structure the way the region is known and valued, particularly for the descendants of those he portrayed as savages. In other words, Darwin has a kind of ethnographic presence in the region—which is both distinct *and* entangled with his biography and contributions to science—because Darwin is alive in the ways Fuegian peoples become subjects in the present.

Today one encounters traces of Darwin at every turn. The southernmost extent of the Andes is called the Darwinian range. One of the highest peaks in Tierra del Fuego is Mount Darwin, a name given in honor of the naturalist's twenty-fifth birthday. The Darwin Sound, which adjoins the Beagle Channel, was named after the young naturalist prevented the *Beagle* from being swamped by a collapsing glacier.[27] These topographic features are important, as they indicate the way in which the history of science, particularly Darwin's legacy, became inscribed upon the landscape.

All this filled Chapman with rage. After retirement, and thus with little institutional support, she spent eighteen years preparing a book titled *European Encounters with the Yamana People of Cape Horn, before and after Darwin*. This is a mammoth book, whose research and writing spans five countries. Chapman meticulously details every single encounter between Europeans and Fuegians, starting with Sir Francis Drake in 1578 and ending with her own fieldwork during the late 1990s. Her stated goal is ambitious and political: "to situate the Yamana and the other Fuegians in universal history as relevant actors during these past four centuries," as opposed to their depictions as "savages, primitives, marginal survivors or exotic curiosities."[28] Yet, as the title suggests, she is mainly concerned with reversing the ways the Yagán had become nearly synonymous with their encounter with Darwin. Her disdain for Darwin is seared into the first page. You can feel it in this passage: "Even the great Darwin referred to them as 'stunted, miserable wretches' . . . who 'kill and devour their old women before they kill their dogs.'"[29] I like to imagine it was Darwin's comment about "their old women" that really inspired Chapman's rage. Her closest Fuegian collaborators were old women. She spent the last years of her life writing an indictment of Darwin. She died at eighty-seven, a year after the book's publication. There is nothing like an old woman's rage to rewrite history.

THE INSCRIPTION PRACTICES OF MUD MEN

Mejillones is one of the most important contemporary landscapes for the Yagán community on Isla Navarino. It is the place where the eldest speaker of the Yagán language grew up, and the place where her body will be brought after she dies. Yagán families were living here in 1907 when Furlong visited Mussels Bay, as he called it. Three years later, John Lawrence, a missionary, rented the land to the Chilean government to establish a Yagán reserve at this same location. In 1958 the reservation was torn down and transferred to Villa Ukika, where members of the Yagán community live today.[30]

One sunny afternoon in the Fuegian spring of 2018, I was driving around with my friend Francisco in his tourist bus, which we were using that day to ferry his extended family, myself, various friends, and their kids out to Mejillones for a visit. Teenage girls were doing karaoke to Justin Bieber in the back of the bus, while we were crowded in the front, drinking *mate*

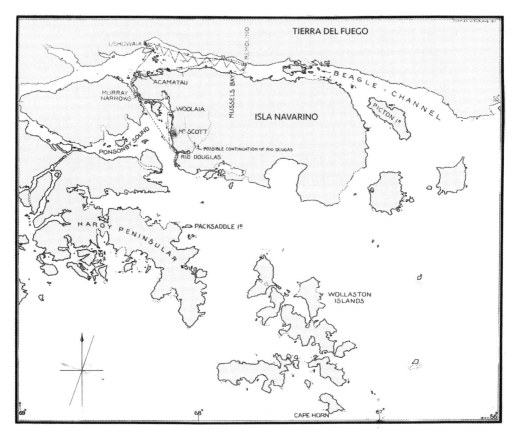

1.6 Modified version of Furlong's map of Isla Navarino, southward to Cape Horn. Mejillones (or Mussels Bay) lies on the Beagle Channel, while Wulaia (or Woolaia) is along Navarino's western coast.

and catching up. As we pulled into Mejillones, I said something about how pretty the mountains looked, visible across the Beagle Channel, their snowy peaks vivid against the blue sky and water of the bay. Francisco paused and answered, "Those mountains, well, Darwin was just a terrible person. Really horrible. At least for us. Everything Darwin. It is offensive. For the Yagán, it is offensive."

Throughout this book I use the term *inscription practice* to describe techniques by which an apparatus, such as colonialism, asserts territorial claims.[31] These claims can be made over elements of the earth, such as land and sea; over living beings, both human and nonhuman, as well as claims upon the earth's climate and atmosphere. Birds claim territory through song; fiddler crabs dig burrows; ocean life glows with bioluminescence; beavers build lodges and dams. The suburbs are a nested architecture of inscription practices, from gated entrances to backyard privacy fences. These practices of territorial inscription leave their mark on the world, though sometimes the mark is just a shimmer.

Francisco's comment about Darwin might have been a quick aside, but I don't think so. In his book *Mimesis and Alterity*, the anthropologist Michael Taussig writes that two of the Selk'nam words for white settlers roughly translated to "mud men." These Selk'nam words, according to Taussig, described the ways white settlers covered their bodies with clumps of grass and earth to camouflage themselves during warfare. While these were Selk'nam words, no doubt the colonial killing practices were similar across the archipelago.

In the early 1920s, the anthropologist Martin Gusinde recorded Selk'nam descriptions of colonial mud men at the height of the genocide. About ninety years later, Taussig revisits Gusinde's work in *Mimesis and Alterity*, his brilliant analysis of mimetic magic in the context of colonial violence. Over two decades after reading Taussig's book in graduate school, I stood on the beach at Mejillones, half-remembering Taussig's descriptions of mud-encrusted white men in the Fuegian archipelago. Three generations of anthropologists captivated by the figure of colonial mud men, I thought, as I gazed across the channel to the Darwin range.

When I returned home and read Taussig's book again, I found this stunning detail that I didn't recall: "In order to frighten and intimidate the Indians, the [white] hunters made simulacra of cavalry, mounting on horseback humanlike figures made from earth and grass or from hides."[32] Basically, the white settlers and bounty hunters constructed mud men to frighten the Selk'nam from inhabiting their own territory. These mud men were a form of territorial inscription. Today, wherever you go, the Darwin range looms large, a palpable and constant presence, another form of colonial inscription. At Mejillones, the earth seems to have been remade by and for these mud men.

But the earth at Mejillones archives other histories too, countering the territorial claims of mud men. Down a narrow path that extends up a slight ridge stands a *ciexaus*, a ceremonial domed structure for initiating youth into Yagán learning. Built by Claudia Gonzalez, with architectural advice from her father, Martín, this is the first ciexaus on this land in generations.

Prior to this new structure, only trace memories of ciexaus existed. Much of this memory work has been enlivened by Gusinde's ethnographic

1.7 Ciexaus at Mejillones, built by Claudia Gonzales. Photograph by the author.

descriptions and famous photographs of the ciexaus ceremony, copies of which hang prominently in the town's anthropology museum. Claudia's and Francisco's grandmothers attended the last ciexaus ceremony held at Mejillones in the early 1930s. Claudia's grandmother was too young to go inside during the ceremony. Instead, she stood in the cold, listening to and afraid of the sounds from within.

Francisco brought me here to remind me that some losses are not permanent. At Mejillones, I learned to appreciate how structures like the ciexaus are not just important markers of heritage, culture, and identity; they are also inscription practices that make territorial claims. Building a ciexaus establishes claims in a world saturated by stories of lost tribes and Darwin's looming presence on the horizon.

WULAIA

A few days after our trip to Mejillones, Francisco and his wife, Maria Luisa, invited me to come on a boat trip around Isla Navarino's coast to visit Wulaia Cove. Francisco and Maria Luisa were on the cusp of expanding their already successful tourism business, and this was a trip to introduce Chilean travel agents to important Yagán sites in the archipelago. Their tour boat, the *Alacush* (Yagán for "steamer duck"), has a comfortable enclosed seating and dining area. During our trip, we stayed warm and dry as we cruised through the Beagle and Murray channels, everyone chatting as we passed colonies of seals, while albatross and gulls circled above. In the kitchen below, Maria Luisa and her staff prepared a rich three-course meal for the group, including local king crab, steaks that came from their estancia, and homemade flan for dessert. Alex Hawley, a Navajo woman who grew up in Utah, was my student research assistant on this trip. On the boat, Alex and I were both entranced with wonder, as the boat traveled through glacial waterways so different from the places we each call home.

Once we arrived at Wulaia, Denis Chevalley, a Swiss guide and local historian, described the significance of Wulaia Cove to all of us. Wulaia, he explained, is famous for two related events: here is where Darwin's ship dropped off Jemmy Button and the other Fuegian captives on January 23, 1833, and where, about two decades later, Jemmy Button allegedly led a massacre against a group of British missionaries. This second event is always referred to as the *Allen Gardiner* Massacre.[33]

The *Allen Gardiner* was an 88-ton schooner named after a British missionary who founded the South American Mission Society in 1844 (originally named the Patagonian Mission). Allen Gardiner, the missionary, died years before the ship was built, while trying to establish a mission settlement on Picton Island in 1851. Gardiner chose Picton, which is not far from Wulaia, hoping to make contact with Jemmy Button. He thought Button, with his English-language skills and experience with British society, might prove a sympathetic broker for his efforts with other Yagán groups in the archipelago.

Gardiner and his crew never made contact with Button. Instead a series of escalating missteps proved fatal, as errors tend to compound at the World's End. First, the missionaries had no ammunition, having left it on the ship that dropped them off at Picton Island. Without ammunition, they could not hunt for food. This dire situation became insurmountable when their meager rations were washed overboard as they frantically rowed away from a group of pursuing Yagáns.

As he was starving to death, Gardiner left written instructions urging the South American Missionary Society to continue his work in the archipelago, though he suggested that the Society relocate to the safety of the Falkland Islands. Upon receiving these death-bed instructions, Reverend

1.8 Multiple forms of territorial inscription exist at Wulaia. The large building in the field once housed a radio relay station for the Chilean navy, though it closed in the 1950s. Now a large tourist operation leases the cove from the Chilean government. They use the large building as a visitors' center and built the traditional Yagán domed dwelling (indicated on the left). For the tourists, Wulaia is a stop on the way to Cape Horn and the glaciers. Photograph by the author.

George Pakenham Despard procured a ship (the *Allen Gardiner*) and subsequently established a mission settlement at Keppel Island in the Falklands. For several years, while Reverend Despard was mission superintendent, Yagán families, including Jemmy Button and his family, were brought to Keppel to be taught English and Christian theology, as well as carpentry and gardening.

In 1859 Despard thought relations with Button and his extended family were strong enough to establish a mission at Wulaia. And so that fall Despard sent the *Allen Gardiner* to Wulaia. The ship was loaded down with supplies, a small crew, and three Yagán families who had spent the prior ten months at Keppel. As they disembarked, the ship's captain, Robert Fell, accused the Yagán families of stealing from the crew, and he searched their suitcases. Wikipedia describes this as "a misunderstanding and cultural conflict between the parties."[34] The cultural conflict escalated into a shipboard brawl, after which the Yagán families departed feeling angry and insulted.[35]

Even with this inauspicious start, the missionaries spent the following rainy week building a church on Wulaia's beach. On November 6 the crew ("armed only with the Bible") went ashore to hold the mission's first church service. Alfred Cole, the ship's cook, watched from the ship as the captain and crew were stoned, speared, and stabbed to death. While Tommy Button, Jemmy's brother, threw the first stone that day, most accounts portray Jemmy Button as the ringleader.[36]

Much of what I know about the *Allen Gardiner* Massacre comes from one of Furlong's notebooks, filled with the official testimonies of the event. These testimonies were taken by colonial officials at Port Stanley in the Falklands, shortly after Cole, the cook and lone survivor, was rescued. Jemmy Button's deposition is copied into the journal, as is a letter written by the cook to Reverend Despard. Furlong also transcribed, in his cramped and tiny handwriting, Waite H. Stirling's account of his 1864 visit to Wulaia. Stirling reported seeing the "unmistakable" remains of Captain Fell and Garland Phillips, the ship's catechist. How the identity of skeletal remains could be unmistakable is a mystery. Furlong also drew a sketch of the *Allen Gardiner* in one of his notebooks.

For Furlong, the *Allen Gardiner* Massacre functioned as a kind of colonial morality tale. In this story, Jemmy Button stars as a tragic antihero, representing the hubris of European missionary efforts. Yet, above all, it is the story's association with Darwin, who hovers always in the background, that captivated Furlong. Darwin is a central presence in the Furlong archive. He shows up in published articles and he appears in the typed captions on the back of the archive's photographs. Furlong's notebooks, though written in the field, are filled with Darwin quotes and Darwin facts. These snippets mingle with Furlong's own observations of Fuegian culture and with details he gathered from his missionary informants. When I was transcribing Furlong's notebooks, I often wondered if he carried a copy of Darwin's *The Voyage of the Beagle* in his pack. In his final notebook, written in the field, he describes Darwin's expedition as "one of the most marvelous voyages ever undertaken."[37] With this in mind, it is not a stretch to view Furlong's visit to Wulaia as a kind of pilgrimage.

Over a hundred years after Furlong's visit to Wulaia, I spent several days typing up his handwritten transcriptions of the *Allen Gardiner* Massacre accounts. This was like a written variation of the game telephone. First, a clerk in the Falkland Islands wrote down the testimony of Alfred Cole, Jemmy Button, and other witnesses, men with limited writing skills. The clerk's texts then traveled across the globe to England. There, someone set these accounts into typescript so they could be published in the *Voice of Pity*, the journal of the South American Mission Society (a journal representing the interests of a society forced to defend itself after its second well-publicized Fuegian tragedy). Someone then mailed copies of the *Voice of Pity*, now rare and hard to find, back to Tierra del Fuego. Fifty years later Furlong must have read these accounts while at Harberton, Bridges's estancia, where he painstakingly copied them into his own little pocket notebooks. Reading Furlong's notebooks, I can't tell if Jemmy Button's deposition was fragmentary or if Furlong just grew weary of transcribing the whole thing.

As I sat typing at my desk in rural Vermont, I became one more node in the circulation and accretion of texts that compose Wulaia as a figure. Wulaia has traveled across the world and through centuries, settling here and there, shifting a bit with each rendering. I have no interest in knowing what really happened. Instead, Wulaia has taught me how figures of the present are composed through multiple layers of history, yet these are not stratigraphic accumulations.

THE ARCHIVAL EARTH

At the time of Furlong's visit to Wulaia, Jemmy Button's descendants had largely abandoned their village. In the decade before, Wulaia's Yagán families had moved to the relative safety of mission-associated estancias across the Beagle Channel or to the mission settlement at Rio Douglas, farther along the Navarino coast. Furlong notes this absence in his journals, mentioning, with wonder, that over one hundred families once must have lived here. Still, this was not the loss he chose to memorialize during his visit. Instead, he was so compelled by the story of the *Allen Gardiner* Massacre that he carved and installed a wooden marker at the site where he believed the crew's remains lay in the earth below.[38]

Carving the headstone must have taken some time. Using a pocketknife, Furlong etched these nine words into a wooden plank: *Here lie the victims of the Allen Gardiner Massacre*. He did this, I am guessing, while sitting aboard the *Garibaldi*, a small sloop he chartered in Ushuaia to visit Yagán sites south of the Beagle Channel. So many aspects of this act are odd: the time it took, his compulsion to memorialize, the act's sacred overtones. Furlong doesn't present himself as particularly religious. We know he was obsessed with Darwin, but he makes no mention of Darwin or Jemmy Button in his inscription. So why does he do this?

When Furlong visited Wulaia in 1907, though fifty years after the fact, the *Allen Gardiner* Massacre was still a part of the ethnographic present for settlers living in the archipelago. No doubt these families recognized the growing historical significance of the event (Darwin), yet for the settlers the massacre also held a genealogical significance (kinship). Almost all of Furlong's Fuegian companions and informants were South American Mission Society missionaries or their relatives. No doubt the massacre was part of their shared identity as settlers living at the British frontier of the World's End.

Lucas Bridges, whom Furlong admired above everyone else, was the grandson of Reverend Despard, the superintendent of the Keppel Island

1.9 At Wulaia in 1907, Furlong took this photograph of the remains of a Yagán domed shelter, similar to the one that is there now.

mission who authorized the failed Wulaia expedition. After the attack, in grief and failure, Despard returned home to England. Thomas Bridges, Despard's adopted son and Lucas's father, chose to stay behind. Eighteen years old at the time, Thomas remained at the Keppel settlement, where he continued his studies of the Yagán language and the mission's work. Indicating the massacre's importance to the Bridges family history, Lucas's memoir opens with the Wulaia story. His account follows the conventional narrative arc: the kidnapped Fuegians, Darwin, the massacre. Yet in a kind of apologetic coda, Lucas mentions that his father visited Fuegia Basket, the young girl who was on the *Beagle*, twice in the decades before his death.[39]

At Wulaia, Furlong encountered a territory contoured by histories of living and dying that far exceeded the temporalities of the Darwinian present. While there, he did not feel the *need* to memorialize the loss of Yagán presence, because the traces of Yagán history were overwhelming and impossible to miss. At Wulaia, he found towering shell middens, some thirty feet in circumference, as well as the drag marks made by repeated canoe landings along Wulaia's shore. These drag marks trace centuries of families landing at Wulaia, coming ashore, and everything in between. Furlong cataloged, mapped, drew, and photographed these topographic traces of existence. In the *Geographical Review*, he describes Wulaia's middens in detail: "The mussel heaps of the village site are scattered not only the entire length of the shore of the bay, but are on the landward side of the largest islands. Some of these heaps to the north are at least eight feet high, possibly ten, and could be circumscribed by a circle thirty-five or forty feet in diameter."[40] He goes on to detail everything he found in the middens (from whale bones to a human cranium). These findings convinced Furlong that Wulaia represented the epitome of a precolonial Yagán village. He was so fascinated by this Yagán landscape that as soon as he got back to the *Garibaldi*, he drew a map of the site in his notebook. In the published version of the map, Furlong indicates the locations of the shell middens, the canoe drag marks, and the location of the *Allen Gardiner* grave.

Today the middens and canoe drag marks are less visible on the landscape. Instead the cove looks much like the rest of the archipelago: a narrow strip of rocky beach gives way to several acres of open grasslands. In the background, the Fuegian forests extend up into the mountains beyond. In the middle of the field there is a large red-roofed building, which once housed a Chilean radio relay station.

Yet it doesn't take long before evidence of Darwin's association with Wulaia becomes visible. For example, on one plaster wall of the naval building is a marble plaque commemorating Darwin's visit, installed on the two hundredth anniversary of his birth. In other places there are interpretive signs marking the Darwin and FitzRoy hiking trails.

On the day we visited with Francisco and Maria Luisa, the sky was gray and heavy with damp. The Darwin tributes made me melancholy. Adding to my unease, the decapitated heads of wild boar were skewered on pipes sticking out of the ground near the main building.

Furlong's survey is like a pirate's map written in invisible ink, but in reverse: the ink remains, but the landscape features are gone. About thirty years after Jemmy Button died, Antonio Vrsalovic, a Croatian settler, established an estancia at Wulaia.[41] It appears that Furlong met Vrsalovic during his layover in Ushuaia, a few weeks before. Vrsalovic told Furlong that when he arrived at Wulaia in 1896 there were about ten Yagán people living there, with others scattered about, until they all left the year before Furlong's arrival. In Furlong's photographs, we can see the beginning stages of colonial settlement at the cove. There are outbuildings and scattered fences. Furlong says that the house stands in "what must have been the middle of the village, and the garden soil is composed of their musselheaps."[42]

In the decades after Vrsalovic arrived, the estancia's pigs and cattle uprooted and flattened the land, erasing the dramatic topographic traces of Yagán existence. At Wulaia I learned how colonialism and environmental change are not just contingent processes. Sometimes history, territory, and belonging are transformed in mundane increments. All it took were a few pigs and some cattle, and before long, thousands of years of Yagán history were erased from the landscape.

Furlong's photographs archive the traces of these entangled histories.

1.10 These photographs show the same view of Wulaia Cove, though at slightly different angles. Furlong's image (*left*) shows dramatic shell middens and canoe landing marks. These features are missing from the contemporary landscape (*right*). Right image: Photograph by the author.

1.11   Furlong said this photograph shows "the place of a recently arrived settler," who elsewhere he describes as the "only white pioneer settler" he encountered on the east coast of Isla Navarino. The hills in the image's foreground are shell middens, which extend around and beyond the house. This photo captures the time just before one inscription practice effaced another. The quote comes from the caption of a blurry photograph that Furlong took of Vrsalovic's horse, MSS-197, Box XI, Folder 20, Furlong Papers.

For these reasons, these older images of Wulaia are really significant. They reveal a landscape enlivened by Yagán deep-time assemblages of life. Middens and canoe marks are not kin, but they are traces of kin and being-in-the-world for people who experienced a profound rupture in knowing place through kin.

Though it seems like I am telling a story of the recuperation of colonial archives for other purposes, this would be a tremendous overstatement. Ideas of recuperation neglect the ways colonial archives continue to shape how Yagán people live in the world—as political and territorial subjects of Chile—as well as shape the ubiquitous narratives that continue to consign Yagán existence to the past and to natural history. Once, I asked Serrano if using the Furlong materials while collaborating with community members was a way of "decolonizing the archive." He said no, that would be an overstep. In English he said that was "too big an idea." I understood what he meant. Decolonization requires a lot more than writing books and plundering archives.[43] At the World's End, Darwin and his fellow mud men became sea and mountain. Cows and pigs remade the land in ways that silence other histories and territorial claims. And yet, although the earth may be silenced, it remains an archive of histories and temporalities that continue to shape existence in the world. The entire coast of Isla Navarino is hilly with histories of living that exceed colonial inscription practices.

Arturo Escobar · *A Figure*

F3.1 Eva Kelly and Arturo Escobar, walking in Everglades National Park, 2012. Photograph by Ulrich Oslender.

I have a photograph of Arturo Escobar walking barefoot in a mangrove swamp in the Florida Everglades. This was the first day I met the cultural anthropologist. In the photograph, he is following my daughter, Eva, who was about six years old at the time. She too is barefoot, her pink skirt hiked high above her dirty legs. They are both laughing with the joy of feet squishing in the algae-encrusted mud. Here, the earth is always in a state of becoming liquid. On that day, I remember Arturo mentioning how much these mangrove forests reminded him of the Pacific coast of Colombia, the landscape that taught him so much about the complexities and politics of being deeply rooted. His book *Territories of Difference* is where I learned to pay attention to the politics of nature, coloniality, and earthy modes of resistance.

In English, there are so many unflattering references to mud: "Stuck in the mud," meaning unable to complete a task, and "Stick in the mud," meaning conservative and boring.[1] Yet mud resists the lure of endless forward momentum. The lure of endless forward momentum comes in many guises, as Arturo has shown: development, sustainability, modernity, globalization, to name a few. But the muddy earth, literally and figuratively, slows things down. Mud is antimodernity. Mud holds place and territory dear. Mud is the earth's version of resistance. Mud archives overlooked histories.

Mud is a life project, too. Challenging our basic understandings of what constitutes living, mud teems with sulfuric, anaerobic life. Bacteria, crayfish, worms, and the like flourish in the muddy earth. Tiny creatures create subterranean burrows in the mud, a meshwork of sorts, which enable oxygen and nutrients to cycle across multiple strata. In its solid form, mud creates architectures of life and loss, from sunbaked adobe walls to funereal urns. Muddy floors are a vexing reminder of the futility of keeping nature out. Muddiness by definition is an ontological mess: land or sea, earth or water, nature or culture?

Yet this ontological shiftiness enables the muddy earth's radical potential. Mud could be mistaken as life at the slow margins of the world (particularly by those entranced by the lure of endless forward momentum). Things slow down when you share instant coffee at a community center on the Mississippi Bayou or when you are riding the deep muddy trenches of the road to Huehuetenango. Yet mud worlds are assemblages sustained by long-term practices of living collectively with other beings and things. Territoriality, as Arturo makes clear, is a form of politics and knowledge that builds over time, in place. Staying attuned to the earth, he argues, is foundational to relational politics and transitional thinking.[2]

Mud men, such as Charles Darwin, have left their traces upon the archival earth. Yet, as Arturo and my Fuegian collaborators have taught me, strength and wisdom come by staying connected, holding firm, even in the face of one more assault on the integrity of difference. All it takes is one storm too many to unleash mud's terrific potential.

The Archival Earth · *A Figure*

F4.1 Furlong began his Fuegian expedition in the town of Ushuaia, which is visible across the bay in this photograph. From Ushuaia, he chartered a sloop to explore the waterways and islands south of the Beagle Channel. Once a Yagán population center, Ushuaia was a penal colony and frontier town with about three hundred permanent residents in 1907. The image's foreground shows the skeletal remains of the South American Missionary Society's first Fuegian church, established in 1870. The Darwin range is in the background. Photograph by Charles Wellington Furlong.

Furlong's photographs capture the ebb and flow of colonial inscription practices as they transform land and sea into the World's End. I could stare at his portrait of Ushuaia for hours, trying to make sense of the heterogeneous temporalities the image reveals: mountain time, tree time, the lifespan of a mission, and so many more. Aware that he was witnessing the emergence of "civilization" at the frontier, Furlong also was keen to document a future in the making. The earth archives all of these temporalities and inscription practices, though they are largely absent from the "archival earth," as one of the dominant figures of our time.

Earth system scientists are calling on concepts from geologic time to support efforts to designate the Anthropocene as a formal unit of earth history.[1] For the scientists leading these discussions, such as scholars associated with the Anthropocene Working Group, the present is the result of fossil fuel technologies, transportation and communication networks, population growth, as well as escalating consumption patterns. These are uneven modes of proliferation, even as their traces are globally distributed. More recently, and in response to critique, this community has been careful to acknowledge the Global North's disproportionate responsibility for processes of global environmental change.

For Anthropocene scholars, the earth archives the present and the present emerges in stratigraphic time.[2] Stratigraphic time is deep time; it is unidirectional and cumulative. Stratigraphic time builds like layers on a cake, though it does so at a geologic pace. In the geologic time scale, a million years hardly registers in the grand scheme of things. This is not a "snail's pace." Instead, stratigraphic time accrues in increments outside the experience of an individual or a generation and is beyond the temporality of a species. After all, snails come and go within the Holocene, as the fossil record makes clear.[3]

Perhaps because the slow temporalities of stratigraphic time are hard to comprehend, layers of the earth have become a proxy for knowing slow time. Stratigraphy's fundamental insight is the Law of Superposition, which assumes that layers of sedimentary rock form on top of older layers.[4] This seemingly simple insight allows geologists to read the earth's layers as time. With stratigraphic time, the earth feels like it is getting larger and larger through time, like a round candle being repeatedly dipped in wax. This is the bedrock of stratigraphic time (excuse the joke): one unit of time does not replace the prior, like changing clothes before a party. Instead new periods of time settle as sediments. Stratigraphic time is a geospatial rendering of time, a geochronology, that is slow and steady, unidirectional, yet global in its reach.

According to the logics of stratigraphic time, the earth itself has become the most compelling archive of the present. The earth archives plastics, concrete, nuclear fallout, black carbon, and agricultural fertilizers, among other industrial materials. All of these serve as trace evidence of a world distinct from the Holocene.[5]

Of particular note is the role of plastics in the stratigraphic record. Plastics persist with a temporality that seems to mirror the geographic time scale. Environmental scientists have long been concerned about the impacts of plastic pollution on the health of ecosystems, humans, and other species. Chemicals in plastics disrupt endocrine systems, affect reproduction, and cause cancer. Most of us have phthalates, used in vinyl flooring among other things, in our bodies, and bisphenol A in our urine.[6] Marine birds and mammals become tangled in discarded plastic strapping, or they starve when their guts become clogged with plastic fragments. Still, these "transformative changes" do not make the stratigraphic present. This is the reason earth scientists are making the case that plastic should be reconceptualized as a "geological material." This reconceptualization would allow plastics to be used as a stratigraphic marker of our current time. Plastics have been found in every nook and cranny of the earth, even in the remote seas of Antarctica.[7]

Yet Antarctica archives more than just plastics. In an important paper published in *Nature*, Simon L. Lewis and Mark A. Maslin argue for an Anthropocene start date of 1610 based, in part, on a global reduction of atmospheric CO_2 found in high-resolution Antarctic ice cores. As their paper suggests, these ice cores vividly illustrate how the earth's stratigraphy archives losses beyond that of environmental change. The authors use the term *Orbis spike* to refer to several strands of evidence that show the ways in which colonial encounters, genocide, and biotic exchanges reconfigured the earth after 1492.

The carbon story Lewis and Maslin offer is counterintuitive: colonial genocide in the Americas led to a significant pattern of forest regrowth, at least in the first century or so. This dramatic depopulation, with an estimated loss of 90 percent of Indigenous peoples, also meant that forest clearing and burning for farming and hunting were dramatically reduced. The subsequent continental-scale reforestation of the Americas enabled the increased sequestration of atmospheric CO_2. The resulting reduction in atmospheric CO_2, they argue, is the "most prominent feature" in the "pre-industrial CO_2 records over the past 2000 years."[8] Or, in Heather Davis and Zoe Todd's words, the ice cores show how "rock and climate are bound to flesh."[9]

At its most obvious, the ice cores of the Orbis spike tell a stratigraphic story. While this is an important intervention into the environmental history of the earth, stratigraphic time has its limitations. For one, stratigraphic time is linear and bound tightly to notions of progress.[10] In stratigraphic time, the angel of history is looking back in horror, yet still comforted with the knowledge that we have moved on.[11] In this case, "we" is the common "we" of imperial modernity. Earth history collapses complicated histories and temporalities into a common history with shared assumptions about the constitution of existence and its temporalities.[12] Within the archival earth, the traces of colonialism are buried deep in the strata, archiving a past that is behind us.

We should be wary of forms of evidence that relegate colonial violence to an episodic past (a carbon dip in an ice core, for example). The stratigraphic version of the archival earth offers a vision of the present that emerges at geological time scales to produce a shared world saturated by loss. But of course, the present is an assemblage of temporalities, some of which do not align with stratigraphic time. The stratigraphic earth cannot tell us about the mixed-up temporalities that shape living and dying as an ongoing imperial project.[13] Neither can the stratigraphic earth show us the ways in which living and dying is a collective enterprise, where boundaries of rock and flesh resist ontological distinctions.[14]

It is not just that colonialism is ongoing, where the twin projects of territorial acquisition and Indigenous erasure continue into the present, as Patrick Wolfe has taught us.[15] But also, the present emerges at the crosshairs of multiple temporalities, many of which resist the forward momentum of stratigraphic time. Writing this book, I learned that the present exists in and through what I call entangled time—time that keeps collapsing back into itself, ensnarling the future in the process.[16] Entangled time complicates and exceeds the chronology of the archival earth, at least in its dominant stratigraphic rendering. This is why Darwin and Jemmy Button keep returning.

2 · ALTERNATIVE ARCHIVES OF THE PRESENT

2.1 Puppup (*center*) and Chalshoat (*far left*), with their families and dog. Of their relationship with their dogs, Furlong said the Selk'nam "treat their dogs well. There seems to be no evidence of how long these dogs have been there or when they came. Undoubtedly, dogs who swam ashore from wrecks were acquired by them." The quote is from the caption of a photograph of two Selk'nam women posed with their dog, MSS-197, Box VIII, Folder 36, Furlong Papers.

EVIDENTIARY SITES

Many evidentiary sites serve as archives of loss and wonder in the present. Here are a few that come to mind.

FUEGIAN DOGS

Dogs feature prominently in Furlong's journals. Selk'nam dogs followed close as Furlong's party forged streams and rode through the thick Fuegian forests. Sometimes these dogs tracked guanaco or other game. Each night, the dogs slept warmly with the Selk'nam guides and their families—dogs and babies snug together. Furlong thought these dogs descended from European breeds, survivors of past shipwrecks. He was probably wrong about this, as there were dogs in Fuegia well before the arrival of European ships. "Fuegian dogs," as they are now called, descended from the local culpeo fox (*Lycalopex culpaeus*). These dogs lived and hunted with Yagán and Selk'nam families on islands throughout the archipelago. Now extinct, one of the last specimens was collected at Rio Douglas, on Tierra del Fuego, in the heart of Selk'nam territory.[1]

Today's Fuegian dogs are Patagonian variants of imported working dogs, mainly Australian kelpies and border collies. These animals seem to have sheep knowledge inscribed into their DNA, though the horse-dog-human collaboration central to estancia life requires years of training and becoming together in the work of sheep. In his journals, Furlong expresses admiration for the herding dogs he saw on the estancias, though not because of their unique skills and work ethic. Instead, Furlong was impressed by the dogs' profound attachment to sheep. He describes estancia puppies sleeping "in a nest of wool" while being suckled by ewes. Fuegian dogs archive complex multispecies relationships, including centuries of work and global connection, as well as histories of loss and wonder.

THE FURLONG PAPERS

Derrida begins his book *Archive Fever* by tracing the Greek etymology of *arkhē*, a word that evokes a sense of gathering (the gathering of signs) as well as control over the gathering process. For Derrida, these are not distinct principles in the logic of the archive. Instead, how and what gets gathered and the jurisdictional authority over the process are bound up in the archive's institutionalization. These logics exceed the archive's origins.[2] This is an important prism for understanding the institutionalization of the Furlong Papers at Dartmouth College. Dartmouth was founded in 1769, ostensibly for the education of Native American students on unceded Abenaki territory along the Connecticut River.[3] The archive "forgets," as Derrida tells us, its jurisdictional origins. Most origin stories require some forgetting. Dartmouth's origin story cannot be disentangled from the imperial loss and wonder logics that led Eleazar Wheelock to establish the college at the wild frontier of the English colonies for the education (assimilation) of Native peoples, though we often forget this. The Furlong Papers sits amid this institutional history like a nesting Russian doll.

NATURAL HISTORY MUSEUMS

While natural history museums once archived exoticized wonders, instantiating imperial, white, masculine optics in the process, today these institutions have become transformed into grief-stricken warehouses of extinct animal and plant life.[4] For example, one of the most astonishing rooms in Paris's *Grande Galerie de l'Évolution* is a cavernous arcade of skeletons and taxidermy. A stern and lonely-looking mountain gorilla stands sentinel over a vast array of extinct animals, including a dodo from the island of Mauritius. Across the globe, in Auckland's War Museum, several species of flightless birds are encased in glass. Above all these loom the extinct moa, twice as tall as a person and as fantastic as a unicorn. It appears that New Zealand's flightless birds never had much of a chance, at least after the first wave of human settlement on the islands.[5] In North America, New York City's Museum of Natural History displays a specimen of the Tasmanian tiger, a now-extinct carnivorous marsupial. Internet chat rooms document possible sightings of this wiry animal, keeping hope alive that a few of these "tigers" managed to evade the last of the Tasmanian bounty hunters.

ZOOS AND SEED BANKS

Benjamin, considered the last of the Tasmanian tigers, died of exposure in 1936 after being accidentally locked out of its enclosure one cold night at the Hobart Zoo.[6] Zoos are other evidentiary sites of loss and wonder, often becoming last-ditch asylums for endangered species and their genes, though, as Benjamin's case suggests, not always successfully. Several famous "endlings" died in zoos, such as Martha, a passenger pigeon, and

Incas, a Carolina parakeet (both at the Cincinnati Zoo).[7] Like zoos, seed banks have become the holding grounds for botanical diversity, as climate change and monocrop agriculture threaten the earth's plant diversity. The most famous of these, the Svalbard Global Seed Vault, resides on the frozen Norwegian island of Spitsbergen and archives nearly a million samples of seeds, all wrapped in little foil packages.[8] Other efforts, such as the Frozen Ark in the United Kingdom, archive the genetic material of endangered animal species, with an eye toward a future that has been reanimated by lost or nearly lost species.[9]

A LETTER TO THE KING AND QUEEN OF NORWAY

In May 2019 friends sent me a video of Yagán protestors confronting King Harald and Queen Sonja of Norway. The Norwegian monarchy were in Puerto Williams as part of a state visit to Chile, where they were representing the interests of Norwegian salmon farms and other businesses. In the video, Abuela Cristina Calderón, the community's respected elder, David Alday, the president of the community, and Alberto Serrano, the director of the anthropology museum, greet the king and queen. Behind them is a large crowd, chanting and holding signs that read "Yagán Territory without Salmon Farms." News outlets reported that these protestors had attacked the monarchy's car.[10] The protests spread to mainland Punta Arenas and Santiago and received international press coverage. While there were many profound aspects to this protest, President Alday's letter to the king of Norway stands out.[11]

In the letter, Alday first establishes Yagán territorial claims and obligations to the Beagle Channel: "We, the Yagan Indigenous Community, the southernmost native people in the world, want to give you this letter, as for thousands of years we have cared for our environment in this southern place."[12] Throughout the letter, Alday insists on presenting the archipelago as a landscape that archives Yagán history and culture, where "every shore regards and tells about our presence in these islands, how we lived and persist in such an extreme and cold place." It is this territorial connection, Alday asserts, that explains their ethical obligations to the Beagle Channel as "canoe people."

As Alday's letter makes clear, the Beagle Channel also archives decolonial resistance.

After detailing the salmon industry's devastating environmental record, Alday insists that their rights must be attended to "after the awful and dif-

2.2 Abuela Cristina presenting the letter to Queen Sonja of Norway. King Harald is on the front, right side of the photograph. David Alday, wearing a black "Territorio Yagán" sweatshirt, is in the middle, with Alberto Serrano standing behind him. During this meeting, Abuela Cristina reiterated that she did not want salmon farming to harm her family and people. Photograph published in *Patagon Journal*, April 5, 2019.

ficult situations our people have passed through over the centuries." The refrain of Yagán resilience appears again at the letter's end, where Alday says the community is "still resisting the consequences of the colonization process."

Alday recognizes the World's End politics at play in this debate. He describes how ideas about uninhabited frontiers enable current exploitation of Fuegian life and sovereignty:

> Salmon farming expansion in our waters is not because of the industry success, instead it is due to the absolute failure of it. For decades, this environmental catastrophe has been taking place, where complete regions are destroyed and their people put in harms way. *Now, they are searching for new waters, new places to expand this disaster* [emphasis added].
>
> And for this we haven't been consulted. No one asked our people about this, despite the existence of international agreements that compel the Chilean government to do so. . . . By law we should have been asked; instead we are absolutely ignored. Again, we are not respected.

In Alday's analysis, the World's End is a place and a people beyond the care of the Chilean state.[13]

MY COUSIN'S PANTRY

Of course, there are many more mundane evidentiary sites that serve as archives of the present. For example, several years after my mother died, I had to return to her hometown of Arcadia, a dusty place in central Florida's cattle country. Everything about this trip was heavy with the unresolved weight of our uneasy history. More immediately, the bankrupt managers of the local cemetery never installed my mother's gravestone, and they also buried her ashes in the wrong spot. My cousin Debbie was well-connected in Arcadia, having stayed enmeshed in the network of obligations that accrue when you descend from the town's earliest white settlers. Her reputation for toughness, which just straddled the safe side of acceptable, also explains how she convinced the cemetery management to "put things right."

My best friend, Gina, came with me on this trip, having visited Arcadia once before, the summer we were fourteen and I was learning to microwave food for my dying grandmother. Needless to say, sometimes it helps to have a friend with you. After our morning meeting at the cemetery, Gina and I returned to Debbie's house for a visit. Debbie lived in an enclosed and air-conditioned section of her barn, sleeping within earshot of her prized Tennessee Walkers. In addition to training hunting dogs and horses, Debbie was now leading "prepper" courses which she advertised on Facebook and several conspiracy-oriented webpages. I remember Gina and I listening as Debbie explained how more and more city people needed to know how to kill and prepare a deer, smoke their own meat, and can vegetables. She said, as we peered into her kitchen pantry, "With this global warming, things are going to go south real fast." Inside the pantry, homemade canned goods were stacked from floor to ceiling, dusty with the anticipation of the coming apocalypse.

Lichens on the Beach · *A Figure*

F5.1 Orange lichen on the shore of Isla Navarino, overlooking the Beagle Channel and the Darwin range of the Andes. Video still by Christy Gast.

Darwin certainly must have noticed the brightly colored bands of lichens that cover the rocks along the Fuegian beaches. From the air they look like someone has splashed orange or white paint along the shore, offering a stark contrast to the changing blues of the adjacent sea. Up close, many of the rocks and boulders are fully encased in lichen species, while in other areas the lichens grow in crystalline patterns that spread out across the rocks' dark surfaces. In this landscape, lichens are one of the few creatures that can hold their own against the tides, salt spray, and the sub-Antarctic's frequent storms. In some ways this is not surprising, as lichens appear to thrive in difficult conditions. For example, some orange sunburst lichen (*Xanthorium elegans*), a near relative of those in the photograph, managed to survive eighteen months while attached to the outside of the International Space Station.[1]

There is a predictable pattern to the form and territorial extent of Isla Navarino's coastal lichens.[2] For the most part, each color of lichen represents a different species. In turn, each species claims its territory by growing in different colored bands that extend up from the water to the very edge of the splash zone. First, and regularly submerged by the tides, is a zone of black or purplish lichen (*Verrucaria*) that extends out from the water to reach the high-tide line. Abutting this black lichen zone, and in magnificent contrast, are various species of electric-orange lichen (*Caloplaca*). A few meters above sea level, white or cream-colored lichens of several genera rise above the orange lichen like the frosting on a psychedelic layer cake. This layering of black, orange, and white occurs in polar regions throughout the world.[3] The central tendency of these species, like a territorial signature, appears to be motivated by relative tolerance of specific lichen species to saltwater.

Lichen ways of inscribing territory seem more benign than those at play in the apparatus of settler colonialism, though they are also colonizing assemblages of life. Perhaps it is because lichens are relational beings, composed of not one species but at least two (one or two types of fungus paired with a cyanobacterium or an alga), while hosting a profusion of other species in their thallus.[4] Anne Pringle has said that while we still have an imperfect understanding of lichen's natural history, "it is clear that lichens are worlds unto themselves."[5]

Over the centuries, lichens have posed a considerable taxonomic challenge. Early theories suggested they were the "excrementitious matter produced by the earth, the rocks or the trees," or perhaps the result of plant decomposition.[6] The collective nature of lichens presented an uncomfortable problem to nineteenth-century scientists used to approaching life through

Darwinian models of species competition. Simon Schwendener, a Swiss botanist, first identified the "true nature of Lichens," though he envisioned the fungal-algal relationship as akin to that of master and slave.[7] Instead, it appears that lichens live symbiotically, a model of cohabitation and collaborative existence.

Lichens have lived on earth for much longer than other forms of life, predating plants by about 200 million years. Lichens live a very long time—hundreds to thousands of years. That, coupled with their slow growth rate, have made lichens an important resource for archiving history, loss, and change. This is particularly true of crustose lichens that grow radially over substratum, such as those found on the rocky shores of the Fuegian Archipelago. Some crustose lichens found in the Arctic may live to be over five thousand years old, "making them candidates for oldest organism on Earth."[8] Lily Lewis, a scientist who has done research throughout the archipelago, described Isla Navarino's lichen and bryophite species as "sisters" to those in the Arctic, though she cautions that we know much less about Fuegian species' varieties, age, and diversity.

It was this compelling sisterhood of relational living that led Christy Gast, Camila Marambio, and I to investigate lichens on Isla Navarino. While there, we spent hours filming lichens in the forest, on the beach, and in the peat bogs. We talked to lichen scientists and lichen lovers. We also photographed different lichens using high-spectrum microscopes at the Omora Field Station's laboratory in the town of Puerto Williams. Mainly, we spent a lot of time thinking with lichens.

It is safe to say that Isla Navarino's larger crustose lichens have witnessed histories of enormous change. A half-century ago, a graduate student named Roland Beschel developed a method for dating rocks using lichens by measuring the growth rates of lichens on tombstones in an Austrian cemetery.[9] The dates on the tombstones helped Beschel estimate when the lichens became established on the stone's surface. From that, he was able to determine a relative growth rate for lichen, allowing him to substitute lichen size for time. More recently, the mycologist Anne Pringle has theorized that the fungi in *Xanthoparmelia* lichens growing on New England gravestones are immortal.[10] Countering expectations about plant and animal lifetimes, Pringle's research suggests that as lichens age and grow they become more resilient and actually reproduce more. In cemeteries throughout the world, lichens and tombstones overlap to inscribe different forms of being in the world. Lichen times and human times diverge, though on gravestones the traces of their inscription practices mingle.

F5.2 Lichens obscure colonial inscription practices. The gravestone, in the English Cemetery at Estancia Caleta Josephina on Tierra del Fuego, was inscribed, "This Stone Was Erected by Their Fellow Employees, in Memory of Edward Williamson and Emilio Traslavina, Who Were Killed by Indians, near San Sebastian, January 16th 1896." Photograph by the author.

In 1690, long before Darwin's arrival, George Handisyd, a British surgeon in the Royal Navy, collected lichens along the Strait of Magellan.[11] These specimens, now housed at the Natural History Museum in London, represent the first botanical collection from the region. When Darwin arrived on the coast of Tierra del Fuego in 1830, accompanied by the Fuegian captives, he may have walked right over the very lichens that enliven the beaches of the Fuegian Archipelago today. Certainly this walk was a consequential moment in the making of the present, though no traces of his presence are left on the lichens' surface. Lichens remind us of the heterogeneous temporalities of living, dying, and enduring at the World's End.

3 · AN EMPIRE OF SKIN

3.1
From Lewis H. Morgan, *The American Beaver and His Works* (1868), plate 1.

KILLABILITY

We traveled to Chorillo los Perros, a small creek running through Tierra del Fuego's dark forests, to immerse ourselves in the world of beavers. Christy Gast, Camila Marambio, and I were a part of a group of artists and scholars invited to Karukinka Nature Park to contemplate the role of beavers in the transformation of the Fuegian landscape.[1] At this little creek, silvery timber and broken tree limbs are scattered about like desiccated pick-up sticks. Once, this wide valley hosted a rushing river. Now the thatched mud dams of beavers have slowed this river to a steady soft trickle. Adjacent to these dams, beaver lodges rise high above the water line. We spent a lot of time here, as well as in other parts of Karukinka's forests, learning about the politics, ethics, and impacts of animal life considered invasive and destructive.

Furlong visited this forest in 1907. His journals provide some insights into how this forest must have looked at the time. After a difficult two-day ride over mountains and through peat bogs, he spent a restful night here. In the morning, he lay awake a long time, "watching insects, birds and looking up through the beautiful green tracery of the beeches."[2] This forest was one of Furlong's favorite places in the archipelago.

Little of Furlong's Edenic forest remains here now. About forty years after his visit, the Argentine government introduced beavers into the Fuegian Archipelago, as I describe in this chapter. In this short span of time, beavers have become one of the most dramatic agents of loss in the region. Ecologists believe that beaver families now reside in about 98 percent of all the rivers and streams on Tierra del Fuego and can be found on the majority of other islands in the archipelago. Except for packs of wild dogs, very little seems to slow the steady expansion of the animals into new territories.

Scientists use the term *ecosystem engineer* to describe how beavers transform landscapes by building dams in rivers and streams. These dammed rivers flood the surrounding areas to form ponds, where beavers then build their mounded dens to be safe from predators. For environmentalists, beavers in the archipelago are out of place, threatening, and symptomatic of devastating loss. Their proliferation has led to wide-ranging patterns of deforestation, alterations in native waterways and watersheds, as well as shifts in nutrient and chemical cycles. Ecologists have compared the impacts of the beavers to "the retreat of the last ice age," a phrase that reminds me of the ways evolutionary time has become entangled in the present.[3] Beavers make sodden worlds of smothered roots and submerged life.

3.2 Chorillo los Perros, Karukinka Nature Park. Photograph by Christy Gast.

Forest trees in the archipelago are less adapted to flooding. There is enormous uncertainty about the rate of forest regeneration, a grave concern to environmentalists and scientists. Guillermo Martínez-Pasture, a forest scientist for the Argentine *Centro Austral de Investigaciones Científicas*, told me that beavers have caused the loss of about half the riverine forests in Tierra del Fuego, and the center's studies suggest regeneration may take a hundred years in the flooded areas. The refrain of uncertainty reverberates in discussions with environmental scientists, as forest loss caused by widespread flooding is without analogue in the Fuegian Archipelago.

Like many people, my feelings about invasive species are filled with contradictions.[4] Put bluntly, "invasive species management" entails killing any plants or animals considered out of place and unruly. The ethical justification of this killing, or what posthumanist scholars have called killability, rests on a paradigm of nature that sees the world as fairly static.[5] Killing is justified because invasive species produce change at an unnaturally accelerated rate, a rate outside the slow pace of evolutionary time. While these logics make no sense to me, I simultaneously share a desire to halt the spread (even kill) particular examples of plants and animals that are transforming landscapes I love (for example, the giant pythons that are gobbling up all the rabbits and other small mammals in the Florida Everglades).

To grapple with my contradictory feelings, I decided to investigate this issue ethnographically. Though I had worked for over a decade in the Florida Everglades, a place famous for its invasion problems, investigating this topic there was not a real option. I was simply too close to the Everglades to move beyond the rigid logics of the invasive species paradigm. In the year I started this project, for example, endless stories of pythons filled the evening news, as legislators debated curtailing the exotic pet trade. That same year, my family's farm at the edge of Everglades National Park became ground zero for a tegu lizard invasion. These caiman-size reptiles, originally from Argentina, established themselves in the roots of our backyard avocado grove. A tegu ripped our basset hound's ear during a fight. Another time, we found a cat's body, torn apart, in the yard. I had to give my chickens away. The invitation to do fieldwork on beavers in Chile was a godsend.

In some quarters, the killability of Fuegian beavers is astounding in its everyday articulations. As an example, my research assistants, Derek Corcoran and Giorgia Graells, told me this story: A few years ago they were giving a talk to schoolchildren in Porvenir, a dusty port town in Chilean Tierra del Fuego that overlooks the Strait of Magellan. Both Derek and Giorgia have done graduate research on the impacts of beavers in the region, and their talk was an informative one about beaver-related changes to the environment. At one point, a young girl raised her hand and said, "My father pours gasoline into their lodges and sets them on fire. Do you think that is OK?"

Other times, the objective language of conservation biology tempers killability's fervor. In these sites, killability is treated as a conservation "problem," where the limits of the problem are defined by the practicalities and probabilities of eradication: different kinds of traps, possible hunting incentives, various biological controls, and the like. No one mentions gasoline. Still, for most lovers of the Fuegian forests, particularly within conservation communities, beavers are killable. In these forest encounters, grief over forest loss determines the ethical boundaries of killability.

ANIMAL DIASPORAS

In 2013 Giorgia drove us through the military checkpoint at Tierra del Fuego's border between Argentina and Chile. As military checkpoints go, this was not an imposing place, just a few low buildings scattered along a rough road. After crossing into Chile, we waited several hours for the Chilean border agents to check our paperwork. It seems the Chilean agents were off having lunch and napping in the adjacent bunkhouse. As we sat in the small waiting room, eating our own lunch, we could see the Argentine agents playing a lazy game of fútbol just outside the window. This was a generative place to think about the problems of militaristic metaphors. And it was here, in the waiting room, that I wondered what would happen if we recast beavers as "animal diasporas" instead of "invasive species."

I recognize the term *diaspora* applied to nonhuman beings produces an uncomfortable tension—one I share. Metaphors of animality have been used to discursively dehumanize people associated with diaspora histories and, by extension, justify colonialization, genocide, sexual subjugation, and structural violence. Applying the concept of diaspora to nonhuman beings also reminds us of how difficult it is to dislodge the "human" as the locus for evaluating all other forms of life.[6] For example, comparing the mobility of animal populations with human populations raises all kinds of questions about nonhuman agency, consciousness, and the cognitive and emotional capacity of nonhumans in ways that mirror utilitarian debates over animal rights and welfare. The unease we feel when extending the concept of diaspora to other beings points to the tensions inherent in an ethics of living and dying where the human is not central. Despite these concerns, my hope is that this unease creates a space for hesitation, allowing us to reconsider the ways in which we value nonhuman life.

There are some superficial resonances between the diaspora and invasive species literatures. Both, for example, investigate processes of population dispersal from a point of origin considered home, though diaspora scholars have considerably problematized return and fixed origin.[7] Both literatures grapple with the difficulties of defining what constitutes shared identity within dispersed populations, including the relative importance and plasticity of biological characteristics in these definitions. That said, the central concern of the invasive species paradigm is to keep nature stable and uncontaminated from messy human entanglements; this is also how the paradigm's adherents justify eradicating life considered out of place and unruly. In light of this preoccupation, anthropologists and other scholars have been interested in how concerns about species "invasions" and nature's stability are marked by racist discourses and xenophobia.[8]

In contrast to the invasive species paradigm, diaspora scholars understand identity, subjectivity, and experience as emergent, as Stuart Hall so eloquently describes, within the continuous "play" of history, culture, and power.[9] Following Hall's refusal to understand diaspora identity as being "eternally fixed in some essentialised past," contemporary diaspora scholarship troubles and resists biologisms of origin associated with scientific racism.[10] As genealogies of the diaspora concept have explored in detail, moving beyond the "homeland orientation" has enabled scholars of diasporas to understand diasporic identity and subjectivity as political and relational.[11] Given its resistance to apolitical biologisms, diaspora allows me to consider how other beings become subjects through exile and other modes of mobility associated with coloniality and empire.

For some scholars, diaspora is mobility violently constituted by modernity's spatial-racial ordering.[12] At first glance, beaver mobility in the Fuegian Archipelago does not appear marked by violence. Instead, the territorial expansion of beavers happens without much fanfare or regard for international borders. For example, a couple of years ago, Christy and I watched a beaver swim across the broad Beagle Channel from Argentina into Chile. The animal came ashore on Isla Navarino's beach, only a few feet from where we stood. After quickly catching its breath, it trudged over to a nearby creek that fed into the channel. Once in the creek, the animal moved rapidly up into the forest beyond. Within a few minutes, it disappeared from sight. This relative ease of movement belies the animals' violent history of imperial displacement.

AN EMPIRE OF SKIN

European colonial settlement in North America was sustained by a ready supply of animal skins, particularly the North American beaver. Like an imperial war machine fueled by beaver pelts, competing French, English, and Dutch trading companies staked claims to beaver territories along interior waterways such as the Hudson and St. Lawrence Rivers. Imagine a network of rapidly expanding traplines, spurred westward by the serial collapse of beaver populations. As Eric R. Wolf shows, this territorial apparatus, centered on an economy of skin, led to the dramatic reorganization of the social, spiritual, and political life of Indigenous communities in the Americas. His work also points to the role of animal life in the production of empire. In this case, the beaver fur trade became the logic and means for world making at the frontier in the early stages of the settler colonial project.

In 1946, decades after the near extinction of beaver communities in North America, the Argentine government imported twenty Canadian beaver pairs to Tierra del Fuego in the hope of establishing a fur trade. Today stocking Tierra del Fuego with Canadian beavers seems like an unlikely economic development proposition. But at the time, Tierra del Fuego's limited infrastructure and connection to Buenos Aires posed significant challenges to the Perón administration's dreams of a united, economically independent nation. From the standpoint of Buenos Aires, Tierra del Fuego was worlds away, a periphery particularly suited to the logic of frontier development strategies. This was also a time when US and Canadian wildlife agencies were restocking lakes with beavers throughout North America, suggesting there was an apparatus in place for handling the logistics of capturing, transporting, and introducing beavers into new territories.

We know something of the beavers' long journey to the Southern Hemisphere. In 1946, Thomas Lamb, a Canadian bush pilot, helped trap the beavers in lakes in northern Manitoba, Canada. Next, Lamb accompanied the animals to New York City by rail, then by air to Miami.[13] There, or so the story goes, the beavers chewed through the wooden door of a refrigerated cargo hold at the Miami airport, causing all kinds of beaver trouble before they were eventually rounded up and loaded onto a clipper ship bound for southern Argentina.

As a frontier development strategy, Argentina's plan to establish a fur trade was not successful, sharing the fate of similar efforts around the world: limited economic success coupled with unwelcome environmental consequences.[14] In this case, the postwar years saw devaluation of beaver pelts, and there was little local hunting or trapping culture anyway. In interviews, people often mention that something about the weather or the terrain in Tierra del Fuego make beaver hides less valuable. I do not know if this is true. Still, with no predators or trappers to impede their progress, the animals quickly began to occupy the region's many lakes, rivers, and streams. Quite soon after their release, the animals crossed from Argentina into Chile, even swimming the frigid Strait of Magellan to occupy the Chilean mainland.

Militaristic and disease metaphors abound in sites where animal and plants are considered out of place and unruly (invasions, eradication campaigns, plagues, and so on). The invasive species paradigm is structured by the politics of racial purity and nationalism, as other scholars have noted.[15] In Chile, *invasion* does double duty. These unwanted animals are often identified as a problem from Argentina rather than as Canadian beavers. For some Chileans, the steady incursion of beavers into Chilean Patagonia resonates with a longer history of territorial disputes with Argentina. Conflicts over Patagonia's geopolitical boundaries arose soon after independence from Spain in 1810, and tensions of these boundaries continue to this day. Across Patagonia, and in Tierra del Fuego, rusted tanks litter the borders, stark reminders of the Beagle conflict of 1978, when jurisdictional disputes over Picton, Lennox, and Nueva islands brought the countries nearly to war.

The beaver fur trade is an old story, one that cannot be disentangled from the transformations of life associated with economic imperialism and colonialism. This framing allows us to think of beavers as diasporic subjects, swept up in tides of mobility and history that complicate static categories of "native" and "invasive." At the World's End, beavers settled in the forest and then in the Fuegian grasslands, locally called the pampas. Here is their story.

FOREST BEAVERS

For good reason, forest lovers are concerned about the impacts of beavers on Fuegian forests. At first glance, Fuegian forests seem simple. There are only a few species of trees here, the lenga (*Nothofagus pumilio*), a member of the southern beech family, being the forest's primary tree species. To survive the strong sub-Antarctic winds, which can blow at about ninety miles per hour, lenga trees grow very close together, their trunks and branches forming an entangled mass. Within these entanglements, lush miniature forests emerge populated by liverwort, moss, and lichen. Some of these lichens may be hundreds of years old, though they are not being swept away as beavers reengineer the landscape. Yet beavers did not settle into an untouched landscape.

When beavers arrived in Tierra del Fuego, approximately forty years after Furlong's visit, they settled into a forest landscape already scarred by the legacies of colonial extraction. While the earliest settlers in the archipelago were British missionaries, Chile quickly began offering vast tracts of land to Chileans and European immigrants, many from Central Europe. Here, as in many parts of the world, the state claimed its territory by deeding land to settlers who agreed to improve the land. Furlong's archive documents these improvements: land clearing, the emergence of new towns, rail lines, and the seemingly endless task of fence building. While in Tierra del Fuego, Furlong visited several sawmills. His journals meticulously detail the labor, technology, and capital expense required to run these operations. He was impressed with the work of these sawmills—and also disoriented. In one passage in his journal, he describes riding through Fuegian forests and coming upon a new mill: "How strange it seems to come suddenly, in the heart of these primeval forests . . . the song of . . . *a mechanical missionary*, converting irregular, beautiful beech trees, which, but a day before, perhaps, were listing to the winds and sheltering birds, into scantlings, posts, beams and sills."[16] Though Furlong's passage is a little hard to follow, I appreciate how he refers to the sawmill as a "mechanical missionary." He was interested in sawmills for the same reason I am. Sawmills were the infrastructure that transformed the Fuegian forest into estancias and remote towns, and by extension, they were the means of inscribing state territorial claims on the landscape. While missionaries capture souls, sawmills capture forests.

Like estancias, forests and sawmills became sites of settler belonging. I thought of this in December 2011, as I sat with Germán Genskowski at his sunny kitchen table, overlooking the western shore of Lago Fagnano in Tierra del Fuego. Germán's family came to the archipelago in the 1880s from Poland. His father, Lucio, worked and lived at one of the last sawmills at Caleta María, a remote location about thirteen kilometers from Germán's estancia.[17] Yet, at its height of operations, in the late 1940s, about a hundred people lived at the site, including the Genskowski family. After the owners closed the operation in the 1960s, Germán's father took over, running the sawmill until 1978. This history, and sense of belonging, was important to Germán, who spoke to me for a couple of hours as we peered over his father's photographs which archive the mill's operation.

Germán was a kind and generous man. The first time I met him, in 2011, he was sixty-six and had spent much of his life attached to this stretch of coastal forest. As we talked that day, his wife, Marisela, fussed over him like a lively bird, making him decaf coffee and adjusting the collar of his work shirt. Near the house, conical bundles of wood lay beneath the lenga forest's canopy. Germán and Marisela lived simply. The house did not have indoor water, and heat was supplied by a hundred-year-old Dover stove. Pictures of their grandchildren decorated almost every surface. During the winter months, Marisela moved to Punta Arenas, a common practice, to be closer to family, leaving Germán alone at the estancia. Before the road was built, the family would ride three days on horseback through the forest to reach the nearest large estancia.

Germán told me a story about the beavers' arrival into Chile in 1962. His father, who was a man clearly attuned to the forest, heard that "little men" were cutting down the forest trees. As Germán told the story, I imagined a diminutive army crossing the border intent on despoiling the Chilean landscape. Germán described the beavers' spread as a plague (*una plaga*), as he pointed to the forests behind us. For Germán, the downed trees that littered the landscape made horseback travel difficult and dangerous. Unlike many estancia owners, Germán had a real affection for the forests and for wood. He was an enormously talented carpenter. On the day we were there, he was busy getting ready for the arrival of a group of twelve tourists, coming for a beaver hunt. At the time we talked, he was killing about four beavers per month, yet he had little faith that the beavers could ever be eradicated.

The sawmill at Caleta María, as well as the early sawmills that Furlong described, also produced timber products for export, such as milled wood and billiard cues. These industries continue to this day, though their scale and reach have grown considerably. Large international timber companies dominate the export market of timber products at the World's End, with mass production of pulpwood, chips, and paper products critical to this market. In 2013 we visited *Forestal Russfin*, a contemporary timber and forest products company in central Tierra de Fuego. The company then was milling about fifty meters of timber a day. The wood was kiln-dried on site, and then used for fine furniture or for finish work in homes and buildings. The company also rented rooms, complete with hot water and satellite television, to tourists who come to fly-fish. In the brochure, a print of the Selk'nam Hain ceremony hangs above a bed.

Russfin's headquarters lies in a section of land that was formerly part of the Caleta Josephina Estancia, one of the earliest sheep farms in Tierra del Fuego. On our visit, piles of logs lay stacked next to various commercial buildings while four semitrucks stood ready to be loaded. I remember thinking about the concept of succession in ecology. We had heard that one of the company guards was a very successful beaver trapper and, unlike the rest of the island, the Russfin's forests were fairly free of beavers. The guard at the front desk told us he had tamed the beavers by feeding them lettuce. These beaver stories, like teeth marks in tree bark, inscribe species presence.

Tierra del Fuego's most famous forest products company arrived in

3.3 Logging on the southern coast of Tierra del Fuego, 1908.

3.4 Lenga logs left behind after the Trillium Corporation went bankrupt and left Tierra del Fuego. Photograph by the author.

1993, when the Trillium Corporation, out of Bellingham, Washington, purchased 400,000 hectares of Tierra del Fuego's forests.[18] Trillium arrived in Chile after weathering intense opposition to logging and other development operations in the United States, with a plan called "Rio Condor" to sustainably harvest the forests.[19] Indeed, the company voluntarily submitted their plans for environmental review and hired environmental consultants, scientists, and foresters to develop sustainable logging plans.[20] Though the company had all the necessary legal permits and funding to move forward on Rio Condor, Chilean environmental activists were able to use the media to cast considerable doubt about the potential environmental impacts of the project and, ultimately, used the Chilean courts to slow the project's implementation and drain the project's financial resources.[21]

Chilean environmentalists simply did not trust Trillium and its owner, David Syre. David and Kay Syre founded Trillium in 1975 as a real estate and construction company, though they expanded into logging during the 1980s.[22] Some of Syre's development projects spawned political dissent, but the company's clear-cutting of forests on Whidbey Island in Puget Sound in 1988 spurred radicalized neighbors to block logging roads and conduct guerrilla tree-planting campaigns.[23] In other words, Trillium became tainted by its association with some of the most dramatic environmental conflicts of the twentieth century, the antilogging protests that took place in the northwestern United States and British Columbia during that time.[24]

In the early 1990s, when the Trillium project was proposed, the Chilean environmental movement was relatively weak after decades of dictatorship during which civil society and NGOs were repressed, and where political discourse greatly prioritized the role of natural resource extraction in economic growth, with minimal attention paid to the environmental impacts.[25] Within this politicized context, halting the Rio Condor project entailed developing connections with international environmental NGOs (such as Greenpeace and the American Lands Alliance), which brought attention to formal political processes, such as agency reviews and litigation.[26] Equally important, at least to Chilean activists, was the emergence of a global anti-Trillium activist network that brought together activists from Bellingham and Chilean environmentalists, both in Santiago and in Tierra del Fuego.

Antilogging activists in Bellingham were aware of Trillium's logging plans in Chile and Argentina and exchanged information about the company and about political strategies with Chilean environmental activists.[27]

Anti-logging activists from the United States provided information about the company's history and helped plan oppositional tactics. The Chilean environmental community was very new at the time, as the environmentalist Ivette Martínez recalled, and so this activist solidarity, from so far away, was particularly important. Toward the end of the fight against Trillium, in 2001, Julia "Butterfly" Hill, a well-known US forest activist, invited Chilean environmentalists to meet with antilogging activists in Bellingham. Later, some of these activists came to Tierra del Fuego to see the forests for themselves.

In the years since Trillium left, Martínez has reconsidered the political context that enabled Chilean environmentalists to halt logging of Tierra del Fuego's forests, and even has sympathy for David Syre, whom she met years later in Bellingham. As she explained, Trillium came to Tierra del Fuego just as Chile was "crawling out of its dictatorship," and Trillium and the forests became captured by environmental, governmental, and international institutions that were incapable of a nuanced approach to forest care.

Ultimately the Rio Condor project went bankrupt. In the process of debt liquidation, the Goldman Sachs investment firm acquired Trillium's Chilean assets at a fraction of the debt's face value.[28] Goldman then transferred the property to the New York–based Wildlife Conservation Society (WCS) for protection.[29] The WCS wanted these forests, which they named Karukinka after the Selk'nam word for *land*, to serve as a new model of conservation, a financially self-sustaining private protected area, with carbon markets as the principal source of revenue (a different form of wonder). Throughout the world, land managers desperately hope that carbon markets will provide funding for the continued stewardship of lands in their care. While beavers were not visible in the fight to stop commercial logging, their eradication is one of the nature park's top priorities. Because trees have an economic value within carbon markets, the impacts of beavers on Fuegian trees can be assessed as lost market value.

Carbon markets are an inscription practice associated with neoliberal modes of conservation. On paper, Karukinka conforms to many of the attributes of a "private protected area," which is often shorthand for neoliberal conservation. The land is owned and managed by an international NGO and thus is not part of the Chilean park system. The WCS can set the terms of access and use of the lands within the park. The WCS shapes the way the land is known and represented to the world. I knew all this when I first began fieldwork at Karukinka. That said, it did not dawn on me that Karukinka was a private protected area when I was there. Nothing about the experience resonated with the weight of neoliberal conservation (or at least what I thought this concept meant). Instead, Karukinka presents itself as a nature park. In the farthest reaches of Chile, a nature park is a fairly modest proposition, even when it is operated by one of the world's largest conservation organizations.

At the time of my visits (in 2011 and 2013), the park was staffed by a handful of Chilean rangers and guards. Bárbara Saavedra, a dynamic ecologist, served as the park's director. The ranger station was in a wooden building; the station's main room was anchored by a large picnic table. Here, visitors and staff drink mate and keep warm near the wood stove. Next to the ranger station is the visitors' guest house (*refugio*). The refugio's kitchen had the feel of a hostel, with years of leftover spices and dried soup accruing in the cabinets. On the floor was a plastic Sprite bottle filled with fuel that we used to start the wood stove. In the main room, I remember a book signed by Isabella Rossellini. Every evening the staff cranked up the generator for an hour to run the computers. The scientific infrastructure at the park includes a shed filled with taxidermy, a few game cameras, some bicycles, and a drone.

Today Tierra del Fuego's forests are marked by inscription practices associated with settler belonging, Chilean state-making efforts, commercial forestry, and conservation efforts, each with their own complex global configurations. Within these, the forest has been and continues to be under threat by multiple agents of change, including beavers. The beaver diaspora's early history maps the ways nonhuman life becomes enlisted into national state-making projects (as pelts, in this case), as well as the unexpected territorial circuits these projects produce. Their story also reveals the ways in which imperial projects accrue over time, like sediment, while capturing different assemblages of human and nonhuman life.

For many environmental organizations and land managers, eradicating beavers in the Fuegian forest is the top management priority. Yet before these forest constituents were worried about the impacts of beavers in the forest, they were radicalized in response to more traditional modes of deforestation. Understanding this forest history is important, as forest beavers live in a landscape configured by extractive capitalism and related environmental politics. In other words, these legacies govern the worlds beavers make and their relationships with other forest constituents ("being beaver," we might say) in ways that are distinct from being beaver in the pampas.

BEAVERS ON THE PAMPAS

The story of the pampas is often told as a narrative of complete rupture. Here is a condensed version: For thousands of years, Selk'nam guanaco hunters roamed the interior grasslands of Tierra del Fuego. Coastal canoe people, on the other hand, lived off the resources of the sea. White settlers abruptly brought these ways of life to an end, transforming the World's End into a productive agrarian landscape, one haunted by the figure of the lost tribe.

Spending time in the Furlong Papers, I learned that this history is not a simple one of abrupt end. Instead, I learned how important Selk'nam and Yagán labor was in the early stages of estancia life on Tierra del Fuego. Furlong's archive documents many aspects of Tierra del Fuego's colonial and environmental history, including genocide. It is quite clear that the Fuegian sheep complex was part of the territorial apparatus that transformed the pampas into a "neo-Europe."[30] Patrick Wolfe describes territorial invasions associated with settler colonialism as "a structure, not an event," though with Alfred Crosby's *Ecological Imperialism* in mind, we see how territorial invasions are also ongoing multispecies processes.[31] Sheep in the Fuegian Archipelago, the epitome of ecological imperialism, also archive Indigenous labor and lives, even as this constitutive history remains invisible in the stories we tell about the pampas.

The first sheep farms in the archipelago were established to support Anglican missionary efforts, though this articulated with the territorial strategies of the Chilean and Argentine states. For example, Argentine president Julio Argentino Roca deeded Thomas Bridges eighty-five thousand acres of land in 1886, in gratitude for Bridges's missionary efforts in service to the nation. This land, once Yagán territory, became the Harberton estancia. Furlong described Harberton as "virtually a small settlement"; it included a boat house, engine room, sawmill, shearing shed, housing for married men, housing for unmarried men, and a cow barn. This infrastructure, all in support of an emergent economy of sheep, was constructed by Christian Yagán workers.[32] At one point Lucas Bridges recalled over sixty Yagán workers living at Harberton. Most of these workers, such as the shepherds, were compensated with "bread, sugar, coffee and clothing," though skilled laborers were paid in cash.[33] The dire need for sanctuary from colonial violence helps to explain Yagán and Selk'nam participation in the sheep complex and settlement at Harberton.

Furlong spent a memorable few days at another mission-sheep estancia

3.5 Yagán shepherds preparing a Christmas barbeque at Laui. Their families are gathered near the canoes, in the background of the photograph. Photograph by Charles Wellington Furlong.

3.6 Yagán shepherds working at Laui, November 1907. Photograph by Charles Wellington Furlong.

called Remolino, a name he translated as "whirlwind." Remolino, owned by Rev. John Lawrence of the South American Mission Society, was just down the coast from Harberton. Furlong spent Christmas with the Lawrence family, which they celebrated by holding a barbecue at Laui, Remolino's shearing outpost and a Yagán settlement. Furlong took a number of photographs that document this Christmas celebration. Beginning at daybreak, Furlong said, Christianized Yagáns began arriving in canoes. Throughout the day, Yagán shepherds prepared sheep over an open fire, and "Yagán turkey," which was roasted penguin. Everyone played games, such as tag. There was a spear-throwing contest. Furlong did stunts, including standing on his head. At some point, a Yagán woman went into the woods, where she delivered a baby.[34]

Like Harberton, the labor at Remolino was supplied by Yagán workers, who oversaw about seven thousand sheep at the time of Furlong's visit.[35] These sheep were spread out at five different camps, two on Tierra del Fuego and three across the Beagle Channel on Isla Navarino. While the winter killed about 10 percent of Remolino's flock each year, it was still a lucrative and expanding business. In the first year, Lawrence doubled the number of ewes in his flock. He was barely able to keep up with the demand for meat and wool, most going to supply the prisons at Ushuaia and sawmill workers.

ESTANCIA LIFE TODAY

All kinds of animal diasporas remake life on the pampas of Tierra del Fuego. Thomas Bridges brought European rabbits over from the Falklands, which spread dramatically, creating an "outbreak" in Tierra del Fuego comparable to the Australian experience.[36] Combating these rabbits by introducing potential predators, including gray foxes, produced a familiar cascade of unanticipated problems. Now gray foxes can be found in greater density in Tierra del Fuego than in the rest of Chile. Later still, the Brazilian *myxoma* virus was introduced and successfully killed 97 percent of the region's 30 million rabbits.[37] In recent years, other animals have settled on the islands, including mink, muskrat, and wild pigs.[38] While the specifics of these animal diasporas differ, in general they are all processes of multispecies mobility entangled in the dynamics of settler colonialism in Patagonia.

Yet of all these animal diasporas, *sheep have been the most significant.* Though Tierra del Fuego may as well be a metonym for isolated wilderness, for the most part it is a working, agrarian landscape. In contrast to

3.7 Sheep waiting to be sheared, Estancia Rio Chico. Photograph by the author.

the island's political boundaries, Tierra del Fuego's ecological zones divide the island horizontally: the Patagonian steppe, locally called the pampas, is found on the northern part of the island, and the mountainous sub-Antarctic forest borders the southern coasts. Sheep arrived in southern Patagonia in 1877, brought up from the British sheep farms in the Falklands. With them came Anglo, Central European, and Chilean settlers and the slow institutionalization of the Chilean state. Since then, the island of Tierra del Fuego has been dominated by sheep, with an average of 2 to 3 million sheep roaming the pampas for the past century.[39]

At the turn of the twentieth century, two large companies managed the majority of lands within Chilean Tierra del Fuego for sheep ranching.[40] Fifty years of agrarian reform had succeeded in subdividing these initial grand estancias into about five hundred smaller ranches, an uneven process Peter Klepeis and Paul Laris argue led to land degradation.[41] Over the past century, changes in market prices for wool and the impacts of agrarian reform have shaped estancia life, though, in practice, the nineteenth-century Patagonian aesthetics and practices of production persist. Life on the pampas, orchestrated around sheep, is figured as essential and timeless.

3.8 Sheep shearing at Estancia Rio Chico (*left*), and wool being pressed into *faldos* (*right*). Photographs by the author.

Contributing to this sense of timelessness, work on estancias is still done on horseback and with dogs, and labor is hardly touched by electrification. At the Rio Chico estancia, for example, we watched as a crew of shearers used clippers powered by air compressors. The shearing shed (called a *galpon*) was loud, warm, and rich with the smell of sweat and animals. The shearers manhandled the sheep as if the animals were drooping mattresses, shearing off the winter coats in thick wool sheets. After they were sheared, the animals, nicked and naked, were corralled outside into a dipping bath. In the galpon, the younger men did the shearing, while others sorted the wool into grades, which were then pressed into square bundles called *faldos*. These operations haven't changed much in the past hundred years, except now the faldos are wrapped in clear plastic instead of burlap, as sometimes people used to cheat and hide heavy objects in the wool bundles to increase their profits.

Sheep are the central organizing principle of life on the pampas. Estancia people think sheep, listen to sheep, and care deeply about sheep. The island's grasslands are fenced and organized into vast grazing pastures and corrals to benefit sheep production. The year, too, is organized by the reproductive cycles of sheep and the production of wool: there are times for lambs, for shearing, for culling, and for artificial insemination. Horses and dogs are entangled in this sheep world. People and their dogs eat sheep at almost every meal. Estancia owners are committed to sheep life as both a business and, for many, a cultural identity.

Like beavers, sheep are entangled in complicated global assemblages of animals, humans, infrastructure, technology, and related discursive logics. Sheep stock is imported from New Zealand, the Falklands, and South Africa, as is sheep sperm. Their wool is shipped for grading in New Zealand, then sold through multinational corporations, and often shipped to China, where the wool is made into sweaters and other commodities. Estancia owners worry about the cost of production, technologies of breeding, and the price of wool and are increasingly interested in new approaches to rangeland management. For example, many of the larger estancias are experimenting with the Zimbabwean ecologist Allan Savory's approach to holistic range management. New rangeland methods are particularly important as the introduced mouse-ear hawkweed (*Hieracium pilosella*) is reducing the forage productivity of the pampas.

Environmentalists worry about the impacts of sheep grazing on the pampas, as well as fencing's harm to the free-ranging guanaco. Yet because estancia life is so profoundly a part of the myth of Patagonia, the conservation community tends to focus its attention on the region's southern forests. On the agrarian pampas, as in other parts of the world, commodified animals and plants are rarely categorized as "exotic," "nonnative," or "invasive," even as they significantly transform local ecologies. In Patagonia, they use the term *baguales* to describe domesticated animals such as dogs and horses that have "gone wild," a category considered ontologically distinct from that of invasive species. As Banu Subramaniam has stated in relation to plants, "As long as exotic/alien plants know their rightful place as workers, laborers, and providers, and controlled commodities . . . their presence is tolerated."[42]

Estancia workers (*ovejeros*) and shepherds (*puesteros*) worry about lambs freezing to death or sheep being killed by predators. Once, when I visited an estancia in central Tierra del Fuego, the manager took us to visit an important archaeological site, Cerro de las Onas. The manager had long hair, short on top, like a rock star from the 1970s. His dog, Jack, a red-haired shaggy fellow, was named after Michael Jackson. Together we climbed up the site's towering rock formations—the wind-softened rocks looked like oversized animals and tables clustered on the horizon. At the top, there was a huge caracara nest. No doubt all the dead sheep below us, many with their decaying hooves still stuck in the rocks, drew this carrion-eater to the site. The estancia manager proceeded to scale the rocks and poke at the chicks with a long stick. Later Derek told me that the estancieros don't like caracara or large gulls, believing that the birds pluck out the eyes, tongue, and lips of sheep when they are in labor. For this reason, estancia people tend to kill the chicks. This belief is old. Furlong mentioned it in his journals a hundred years earlier, as he watched the gulls circling the skies above Bridges's Harberton estancia.

Estancia workers are mainly attentive to working conditions rather than environmental change (at least for now). Estancia life in Tierra del Fuego is isolated and difficult. Most of the estancia workers in Chilean Tierra del Fuego come from Chiloé, reflecting a multigenerational tradition of labor migration from this southeastern coastal island. Workers, many of Huilliche-Mapuche heritage, tend to spend a decade or more on Tierra del Fuego estancias, rarely returning to Chiloé to see their families, living in bunkhouses with a handful of other men. Shepherds, who accompany sheep out to far pastures, live even more solitary lives, spending months at a time at remote outposts, with only their dogs and a horse for companionship.

This was the case for Miguel, who came to Tierra del Fuego as a young man and has been living and working as a shepherd ever since. Miguel is a gentle man, about my age, unaccustomed to company. Shepherds are called *puesteros* because they live for months alone at summer or winter stations (*puestos*) caring for their sheep and dogs. When we visited, Miguel showed us his puppies and the improvements to his living quarters. When he first arrived, puesteros slept on sheep fleeces, piled on the dirt floor of a one-room shack. Miguel said that older puestos are not even fit for horses. That day his quarters were clean and bright. He had a real mattress, a kitchen table, three red stools, and a little storage alcove filled with bags of potatoes. Outside, fresh water could be pumped into a cistern, which was heated on a container attached to the pipe of the wood stove. We sat together and talked of these changes, eating guanaco steaks and *cochayuyo* soup. Still, even with the improvements to his living conditions, Miguel said he was lonely. He no longer goes home because he cannot stand to leave his dogs.

On the estancias, beaver can be a nuisance, though they are not a significant concern. In interviews, if I pressed the issue, estancia owners and workers mentioned the cost and labor of replacing wooden fence posts. Today the fencing crews dip the fence posts in tar to discourage beavers from incorporating the posts into their dams and lodges. On some estan-

3.9 The author in front of a beaver pond on Estancia Marel, Tierra del Fuego. Photograph by Derek Corcoran.

cias, beaver ponds have flooded roadways, creating other problems, though these are all dirt roads, so driving around is not too difficult. If estancia people mention beavers at all, it is with wonder at the appearance of the ponds the animals create—which offer a better supply of fresh water for sheep in this arid landscape.

Much to the surprise of the biologists who study beavers, in Tierra del Fuego beavers have adapted to the steppe ecology of the pampas where sheep roam. It appears to have taken the animals several decades to move out of the forests and onto the pampas.[43] These pampas beavers behave in ways that differ significantly from the behavior of the forest beavers. Pampas beavers eat different foods and use different vegetation to create their dams. On the pampas, they prefer *mata negra* (*Chilliotrichum diffusum*) for their food and building needs.[44] Some dams are made almost entirely of shrubby material and piles of grass, unlike the traditional architectural practices of the forest beavers.

On the pampas, beavers are enmeshed in an assemblage of animal diasporas. Imported sheep drink from beaver ponds; beavers incorporate sheep bones and wool into their dams; sheep alter the vegetation of the steppe, which has in turn altered the construction and eating habits of beavers; estancia workers migrate to the region where they live off sheep and love their dogs; estancia owners come and go, balancing their time at their ranches with other commitments; imported sperm inseminate local ewes; expensive wool travels the globe. Unlike in the forests, beavers in the pampas are not objects of concern (maybe just a nuisance). Here sheep, dogs, shepherds, and now beavers make and remake each other.

SPECIES WONDER

The introduction of plant and animal life is bound up in the apparatus of settler colonialism.[45] Yet, as the beaver diaspora has shown, ecological imperialism is not just the remaking of landscapes to look like Europe. It is also a process of remaking nonhuman life through the constitution of new multispecies assemblages. Pampas beavers seem both the same as and different from the forest beavers. Several generations ago, it was believed these beavers shared a point of origin. In a recent revelation, biologists discovered archival evidence that suggests Tierra del Fuego's Canadian beavers might not have been Canadian after all.[46] Apparently those Manitoba lakes had been restocked decades before with beavers imported from New York, making the Fuegian beavers a mixed lot. As with all diasporas, the question of origin and belonging is troubled by the ways the past and the present remake each other yet still become inscribed in flesh as history and politics.

Animals and plants are captured by the colonial apparatus, often in mundane yet devastating ways. For example, during the height of the mission period, a "fine lawn grass" appeared and spread rapidly throughout Yagán settlements. Thomas Bridges was convinced that this seed was introduced in the soles of used tennis shoes, donated with other items of worn clothing from England.[47] The Chilean state, in another example, asserted its territorial claims to Picton Island in the Beagle Channel by releasing cattle and a few mares there. These animals eventually went wild and spread across the entire island, until the Chilean state granted the Bridges family a concession to the island and the feral animals.[48] Colonial settlement works through animals, at the rough edge of domesticity and wildness.

What this speculative experiment has aimed to show is that the biological species is a limited lens for understanding the ways sameness and difference shape trajectories of loss and wonder in the world. As Anna Tsing has shown in her ethnography of matsutake mushroom worlds, "for living things, species identities are a place to begin, but they are not enough: ways of being are emergent effects of encounters."[49] Certainly the species seems a low bar for understanding the wonder of becoming in forest and pampas. Instead, life springs from the situated practices of beings entangled in historically constituted assemblages. Sheep people, tree lovers, forest beavers, and so on. Rather than some great North American beaver invasion, perhaps we should be considering, with wonder, how plants, animals, and people become through their relations with other beings and things.

I began this thought experiment to help me think outside the boundaries of the invasive species paradigm, not to make recommendations about beavers in Tierra del Fuego. That said, I began this research with the belief that most invasive species management approaches were as arrogant as economic development schemes where live animals are shipped across the globe to start a fur trade. Both projects require enormous efforts at simplification and a related "command and control" approach to nonhuman life.[50] In all honesty, when I began fieldwork, I could not imagine how species eradication or removal programs could be justified. I continue to have enormous concerns about forms of suffering associated with these programs, even the eradication of pythons in the Florida Everglades.

Still, after spending time in Tierra del Fuego, I learned that my own certainties emerged from grief over forest loss and little else. Grief is a beginning, but sometimes it is not enough. Being curious about other assemblages of life, what I am calling wonder, has allowed me to understand that beavers in the forest and beavers on the pampas are not the same. Moreover, the worlds they are helping to produce have very different consequences for fellow beings and environments, including the people who care for them. Holding grief and wonder close is a way of "staying with the trouble," using Haraway's phrase, or acknowledging that living and dying in a time of loss requires much harder commitments than simple managerial fixes or absolution through critique.[51] Our research collaborative has produced films, installations, and performances that seek to inspire wonder at the magic of beaver worlds while simultaneously being attentive to the cascading losses their presence in the Fuegian forests have caused.[52] In doing so, we are not proposing inaction, just making clear how difficult care and action should be. This includes the removal of beavers from the Fuegian forests, which I now support.

The Anthropologist · *A Figure*

F6.1 Charles Wellington Furlong at an exhibit of his Fuegian ethnographic materials, Baker Library, Dartmouth College, December 1962. Photograph by Bruce McPhail.

The invitation to establish his archive at Dartmouth College provided Charles Wellington Furlong with the unique opportunity to curate his own legacy. As we have seen, Furlong's repeated refrain (*the first American and second white man*) indexes key aspects of his desired legacy. Yet this is not the complete story. Furlong simultaneously wanted to be remembered as the world's expert on Fuegian cultures.[1]

In the course of his travels, Furlong collected spear points, bows, arrows, baskets, a cape made of guanaco fur, and enough botanical specimens for four herbariums.[2] His mule, Joe, carried so much gear, including a bulky Edison phonograph recorder, that the poor animal repeatedly (and literally) was bogged down by the weight of his labor.[3]

In his depictions of Fuegian peoples, Furlong cycles between racial stereotypes and sympathetic reflexivity—with confounding rapidity. As an example, his journal entry from January 7, 1908, describes a long, wet day of crossing the thick woods and muddy bogs of Tierra del Fuego near Lake Fagnano. This is early in his travels with his Selk'nam guides, and he is worried about being alone with Aanikin: "As I passed to and from the fire I looked into Aanikin's wigwam, where he lay comfortably ensconced between his wives and noticed that his dark beady looking eyes had been fixed upon me for some time, but it was the wolf-like expression which no white man likes to see lurking in the face or eyes of the savage or man of the wilds."[4]

Furlong's journals are filled with similar passages. This one reads like a surrealist poem composed entirely of racist tropes. While passages like these reveal aspects of Furlong's subject position and its imperial valences, this isn't that surprising. Instead, I find myself absorbed with the mystery of how some of the worst literary conventions of the era ("dark beady looking eyes") become a part of the way Furlong seems to be experiencing life as it unfolds in the field. It is as if he is performing a genre character for a future audience, which includes me.

In the next passage, Furlong overcomes his fear of Aanikin. He forces his way into Aanikin's "wigwam," orders Aanikin's wives to move over, then settles himself down among them. While cozy in the family bed, he commences lessons in the Selk'nam language, which continue for many evenings.

Of course, it is impossible to discern the source and credibility of Furlong's ethnographic information—nor have I tried, as the culture and history of Fuegian peoples is not my story to tell. From his journals, it appears Furlong learned a little bit from his Yagán and Selk'nam guides, such as Aanikin. He also spent several weeks with the Yagán and Selk'nam families who lived

F6.2 Joseph, who carried Furlong's equipment.

and worked at the estancias and missions he visited. Despite the limitations of his research, he increasingly emphasized the scientific value of his ethnographic material.[5]

In Furlong's lifetime, Martin Gusinde, a German priest-anthropologist, was the most famous scholar of Fuegian cultures. After becoming ordained into the Society of the Divine Word missionaries, Gusinde was posted to Santiago in 1912, where he became associated with the Chilean Museum of Ethnology and Anthropology.[6] Gusinde and his museum colleagues, including Max Uhle and Aureliano Oyarzún, focused their work on documenting Chilean Indigenous cultures that they feared were on the verge of disappearing.[7] With this in mind, Gusinde spent twenty-two months studying with Selk'nam, Yagán and Kawésqar families between 1918 and 1924. His first trip, made between 1918 and 1919, covers much of the same territory as Furlong's exploration.[8] Today Gusinde's exhaustive monographs have come to define Fuegian anthropology, and his haunting photographs are even more famous than Furlong's images.

Gusinde and Furlong corresponded for forty years. Their correspondence was formal, though peppered with obligatory wishes of good health, particularly as they became old men. That said, their competing professional agen-

F6.3 Aanikin, second from right, and his wives, Otroshoal (*left*, with child) and Warkeeo. Photograph by Charles Wellington Furlong.

das were a refrain that simmered just below the polite veneer of their correspondence. This was a pattern of exchange that never seemed to change over the years—like the way sibling rivalry becomes the enduring logic of some families.[9] In the early years, Gusinde wrote requesting permission to publish Furlong's photographs as illustrations for his own ethnographic research. Because Furlong urgently wanted Gusinde to acknowledge him as a peer, he obliged by sending dozens of original prints as well as cropping and captioning suggestions.

But underneath this helpful facade, Furlong's letters nag with the desire for scientific recognition. For example, a letter from 1927 includes a variation on the explorer's refrain, though this time he describes his journey as a "scientific expedition": "It might interest you to know that I was the first white man to penetrate the interior of Tierra del Fuego and the first white man to make a scientific expedition alone with the Onas [Selk'nam] through the heart of Tierra del Fuego, some parts of the interior north of Lake Cami [Lago Fagnano] having been penetrated by me for the first time by any white man."[10] No need to psychoanalyze the sexual dynamics of the explorer's refrain here. Furlong's letters offer a portrait of a man trying to reposition himself as an expert on Fuegian culture. In the same letter, he says, as if it is an afterthought, "It occurs to me that you may be interested to draw on some of my material and findings as recorded in publications of mine which I am enclosing."[11] This kind of back-and-forth continues over the next four decades. In his last letter to Gusinde, from 1963, Furlong spends two pages lecturing the Austrian anthropologist on some esoteric point about spelling.

4 · STOLEN IMAGES

4.1 Double exposure, taken near Lake Fagnano, 1908.
Photograph by Charles Wellington Furlong.

At a Yagán community meeting, an older woman said she once saw a jigsaw puzzle of her grandmother's face for sale at the Santiago airport. This was a particularly jarring example of the casual commodification of Fuegian peoples' ancestors and history. Tourist shops in southern Chile and Argentina overflow with postcards and T-shirts featuring the lost tribes' version of Fuegian Indigenous life. Furlong and Gusinde originally took these photographs in the first decades of the twentieth century. While some can ignore the sting of these types of images, imagining your grandmother's face in scattered pieces is another matter.

Furlong's archive contains approximately seven hundred photographs, the majority of which portray Yagán and Selk'nam people. Predictably, many are of people, activities, and objects that were coded as both traditional and precarious.[1] For example, there are photographs of Fuegian people making baskets, sitting in canoes, scraping guanaco hides, and standing in front of "wigwams." Of all Furlong's photographs, about twenty-five are well known and continue to circulate widely.[2] Nearly all of these iconic images were first published in a series of six articles for *Harper's Magazine*, one of the most widely read journals of the Furlong era.[3] At the time, the magazine's readership was safely high-brow and literary, curious about other peoples and their worlds. I can easily imagine Furlong's *Harper's* editions piled up next to a copy of Joseph Conrad's *Heart of Darkness* (1899) in some wood-paneled library of a Boston brownstone.[4]

If imperial wonder is a specific mode of curiosity about other worlds, for the *Harper's* readership precarity is what made those worlds worth knowing. Extinction fears were part of the anthropologist's moral economy during Furlong's era, as other extinction fears are today.[5] Of course, the "vanishing race" motif was hardly unique to Furlong's work. Though I found no direct references to Edward S. Curtis in the Furlong archive, Curtis was a contemporary, and his award-winning images of North American Indians were an inescapable part of Furlong's artist-ethnographer milieu.

The complexities of these tropes are bound up in what the anthropologist Renato Rosaldo has called "imperialist nostalgia," a subjectivity "where people mourn the passing of what they themselves have transformed."[6] Furlong's descriptions of the timeless endurance of "stone-age" man in the archipelago speak to these complexities. Still, there is a political valence to these articles. Furlong urgently wanted the *Harper's* audience to care

4.2 Furlong described this image as Chalshoat's wives "fishing with sharp pointed sticks as spears near Cape Peñas on the Atlantic Tierra del Fuego, 1908."

4.3 Three Yagán girls in a canoe, at Laui, a settlement near Remolino, the home of Rev. John Lawrence. This image was published in *Harper's Magazine* (1909), in an article titled "The Southernmost People of the World."

about the Fuegian genocide. His articles detail the devastating toll of violent sailors and sealers on Yagán populations, as well as the murder of entire Selk'nam communities in northern Tierra del Fuego.[7] He also challenged the governments of Argentina and Chile to establish reserves to protect the Selk'nam, so "this little remnant of people would be saved and the tribe preserved before it takes up the last 'great trek' from which there is no return."[8]

Felipe Maturana, a visual anthropologist, has said that Furlong's "Fuegian aesthetic" became a kind of template for Gusinde and other ethnographic photographers who followed. This template, Maturana argues, extends beyond subject matter and includes, in some cases, identical compositions and poses.[9] This is very true. Even after spending so much time with Furlong's photographs, I have a hard time distinguishing some of his compositions from others' work. Year after year, different photographers and anthropologists took group portraits of Selk'nam families wearing guanaco robes and men demonstrating archery or wrestling.

There are several reasons that Furlong's images became the template for the Fuegian aesthetic, not least of which was his skill as a photographer. Furlong was a painter, with fine art training from institutions in the United States and France. In the years before and after his Fuegian trip, he taught art at Cornell University. This background helps to explain the elegant ways in which he used the polar light to create a contemplative mood in his images, where the Fuegian sky is a brooding, muted presence. He managed to conjure light out of nowhere, as if it was his superpower, and cast it with precision on the edge of a rock or the upturned faces of girls sitting in a canoe.

Reflective light is fundamental to Furlong's most famous image. In it, an extended Selk'nam family walks along the Fuegian shore, their profiles somberly mirrored in the calm waters at their feet. Published in an article titled "The Vanishing People of the Land of Fire," the photograph's allegorical intention is clear.[10] The group seems fragile, marching forward against a vast and bleak horizon, precarious as ripples. Yet focusing only on the obvious refrain of loss eclipses the image's technical wonder. Specular reflection is a magic moment in time when sunbeams hit the water at just the right angle to create a perfect mirror image. Surely specular reflection is an optic for understanding how speculative wonder, even in its imperial form, is central to the Fuegian aesthetics' continued power of persuasion.

At the same time, there are aspects of Furlong photographs that feel

4.4 A Selk'nam extended family traveling along the coast, eastern Tierra del Fuego, near Rio Fuego. This photograph was originally published in *Harper's Magazine* (1910) and is perhaps Furlong's most iconic image.

intimate and spontaneous, as if they were taken by a friend rather than a professional photographer.[11] This intimacy sits in the unplanned details—like Puppup's sideways smile in figure 4.5. These details, often rushed and blurred, are like little sparks of resistance to the Fuegian aesthetic's heavy hand. Furlong's negatives are a treasure trove of such images, jammed together in vaguely labeled envelopes in what appears to be archival triage. In these envelopes, I found a surprising number of double exposures, like the one that begins this chapter. I have stared at this particular negative for minutes on end, yearning for the image to resolve itself with clarity (come into view, become legible). Double exposures register presence and absence simultaneously, like Victorian *memento mori* photographs. In the double exposure, one world seems to be passing away at the very moment another is becoming visible. Yet the negative's mysterious layering is strangely comforting. It seems to suggest that the future is not settled.

4.5 Aanikin, Ishtone, Chalshoat, and Puppup, Furlong's Selk'nam guides, demonstrating archery, January 1908. This photograph is from a series that became the basis of two paintings of Selk'nam hunters published in *Harper's* (1910).

Writing this book, I struggled with the ethics of publishing Furlong's photographs, particularly the iconic ones. On the one hand, the photographs are foundational to the aesthetics of the World's End, and understanding how this repertoire of aesthetic conventions continues to shape the archipelago's figuration is important. On the other hand, the Fuegian aesthetic is filled with so many dangerous omissions. Photography is an inscription practice that works through processes of inclusion and omission, as do other inscription practices. In this case, imperial loss-and-wonder is like a camera's aperture, restricting the trajectory of illumination.

In this chapter, I experiment with "dualphotography" as a model for addressing some of these blind spots. Dualphotography is a photographic technique that records what is in front and behind the camera simultaneously. It is another form of double exposure. I learned about this technique when reading a blog by Tristan Zand, who developed a dualphotography application for the Apple iPhone. Zand made the app because he felt sorry for the photographer who was left out of a group shot. In Zand's mind, these omitted photographers "haunted the scene and saddened it no matter how joyful the capture originally felt."[12] In this chapter, I experiment with dualphotography to show what is behind Furlong's camera, or what is invisible yet haunting the scenes.

ALONE, BEHIND THE CAMERA

Furlong is largely absent from his archive. Even his journals disappoint. Instead of self-reflection, mostly they offer a flat caricature of explorer culture. Figure 4.6 is one of only a handful where Furlong appears in front of the camera. Though I painstakingly removed decades of dust and scratches and generally tried to make the print more legible, it is still a terrible portrait. Even so, it is the best of the lot. In the archive, Furlong is a blurry figure that shadows the image.

For Furlong, as with many anthropologists, being the lone "white man" among the natives was methodologically important. He didn't mind being the shadow figure, as he says in an article published in the *Geographical Review*: "Going alone with the natives has a number of advantages. Two or more white men, speaking a language the natives do not understand, arouse suspicion, usurp much time which should be spent with the natives,

4.6 Furlong is standing on the left with "Old Custan," who wears a guanaco cape, and an unnamed Yagán man, probably William. On the right are the extended Bridges family and friends. Furlong says the photograph was taken by Ellis Briggs in 1932, then the American ambassador to Uruguay. Of Briggs, Furlong says, "He is a Dartmouth man. They live within a 'stone's throw' of the Furlongs." Both images were taken at the Bridges family estancias.

and make them psychologically much less natural. . . . Besides, in exploring alone with natives, one has his ethnological laboratory constantly before him to which he can give his undivided attention."[13] Yet if we broadened the aperture just a bit, we would see that Furlong was hardly alone. Instead, a global network of famous people, well-connected businessmen, missionaries, and government officials enabled the production of his iconic photographs. Even before leaving the United States, Furlong received gear recommendations from Robert Peary, the Arctic explorer whom Furlong described as a "very serious man with iron nerve."[14] In Punta Arenas, the Chilean elite immediately welcomed him, his acceptance facilitated by letters of introduction from US Secretary of State Elihu Root.[15]

While Furlong was in Punta Arenas, the governor of Magallanes arranged for him to catch a ride to Ushuaia on the warship *Presidente Sarmiento*, an accommodation that saved Furlong considerable time and discomfort. Once he was in Tierra del Fuego, a letter from Frederick Cook, another famous Arctic explorer, served as his introduction to Lucas Bridges. This letter helped open the doors and hearts of the entire Bridges family, including Lucas, who became Furlong's most important contact, translator, and source of ethnographic information. The Bridges family estancias, Harberton and Viamonte, served as Furlong's home bases throughout his expedition.

These introductions and their connections were not fleeting. The archive contains correspondence between Furlong and these elite families and administrators that spanned decades, revealing intimate lifelong friendships forged in the contact zone of imperialism. Lucas Bridges and Furlong both became members of the Royal Geographical Society of London; over the years, they met up in London and Buenos Aires. Their postcards and long letters map the ways the Bridges empire expands and contracts during two world wars and over several generations. Furlong also maintained a lifelong connection with Mauricio Braun, the American consul in Chile and one of the most powerful men in Patagonia. Braun hosted Furlong while he was in Punta Arenas, entertaining Furlong as he would a visiting dignitary. In the archive is a photograph of Braun's sons, posing on their polo ponies, playing for an Argentine team called the Penguins.

Aside from the assistance they offered, Furlong really admired the missionaries and sheep farmers he encountered. In his journals, he gushed over their horsemanship, toughness, and general ability to thrive at the World's End. These were his kind of people. He granted special status to settlers he thought had caring relationships with Selk'nam and Yagán peoples.[16] Lis-

ten to the warmth as he describes first meeting Lucas Bridges, writt(
his journal on January 12, 1908:

> He dismounted and greeted me with a pleasant smile and as we passed to the tent he gave an Indian a friendly squeeze about his waist, and laughingly passed his big hand over the long black locks of an Ona girl as she thrust her head out of a wigwam entrance. About 9pm we turned in, the three of us in Despard's little tent. I bunked with Despard in his little wooden bunk, while Lucas lay on the ground. We talked until late. The two brothers about their affairs for a spell, as they only see one another about once a week, and then regaled me with stories of the Onas and his lore. A wonderful pair these men, skilled and versatile in all their undertakings, and with a comradeship for one another fine to look upon.[17]

Furlong's subject position (alone, behind the camera) allowed him to bear witness to colonialism's devastations without revealing his own entanglement within the colonial apparatus. In his journals and subsequent articles, he described settlement as unfortunate, inevitable, and unstoppable. He expressed sorrow and rage over the appropriation of Fuegian lands. He was horrified by the forced relocation of Selk'nam people, including their confinement at the Salesian Mission on Isla Dawson between 1889 and 1911. He knew, too, that the region's vast sheep farms, such as the beloved Harberton, were the major engine driving these changes. As he said in one of his *Harper's* articles, "With the establishment of the first sheep-range, in the early eighties, began a cruel and persistent warfare on the part of the white man."[18]

How do we make sense of this seeing and not seeing? Agamben, the philosopher, suggests that an apparatus is not just a "machine of governance"; it is also a "machine that produces subjectifications."[19] In other words, we are knowing, thinking, feeling, and positioned beings through our entanglements with various apparatuses. If we understand the World's End as a figure of the colonial apparatus, we can begin to consider the ways in which Furlong's photography was part of the imperial machine that produced and enabled forms of colonial subjectivity. According to Zand, the iPhone application inventor, dualphotography marries the image in front of the camera with a portrait of the photographer. This marriage creates a simultaneous record of the scene as well as portraying the photographer's mood and state. If so, then I imagine we would see a man working very hard to manage, perhaps ignore, the contradictions of being alone and enabled by the Fuegian elite.[20]

Stolen Images

NAJMISHK

Furlong spent several weeks at Najmishk, once a Selk'nam village located about a quarter mile from the Viamonte estancia. While at Najmishk, Furlong took many of his iconic images, such as the scenes of Selk'nam on the coast, as well as dozens of other photographs of Selk'nam families. During his visit, there were between eighty and a hundred Selk'nam people living at Najmishk. Many families were living in makeshift shacks (what Furlong called "rancheros"), though others were living in more traditional domed Selk'nam homes (Furlong's "wigwams"). In the archive there is even a photograph of the interior of a large, ceremonial building at Najmishk.

Furlong's time at Najmishk was his most productive. His description of the village is prosaic:

> It was interesting to watch the life of the Indian village at sunset, with the golden light upon the trees, the children out at play, shooting their tiny arrows, chasing one another, the dogs yelping and men and women standing or squatting about within or without their wigwams, while the smoke, curled slowly up toward the patches of clear blue which had now broken through the clouds, which drifted lazily across the zenith. . . . I slept in a wigwam with three Indian men, two squaws, three children and a lot of dogs. One of the women muttered and talked in her sleep a good deal.[21]

In addition to his images, Furlong made several sound recordings at Najmishk, including of Aanikin speaking in Selk'nam, and a recording of a woman magician named Yoyo. For Furlong, Najmishk was the ethnographic epicenter of Selk'nam culture, like a living museum.[22]

At the time, Najmishk was the northernmost territory considered safe for Selk'nam people, though the rough edges of colonial violence were constantly shifting. Just to the north, Furlong reported, the Rio Grande was the dividing line between "the Indian and Whiteman's country," after the Selk'nam had been driven south by the landed elite and their thugs.[23] At the time of Furlong's visit, the Sociedad Explotadora de Tierra del Fuego was the largest sheep company in Patagonia, owning over one million sheep in 1908. Furlong described the economics of this business, saying that each year the company exported six million pounds of wool and over 150,000 sheepskins. Renderers were able to produce about fifteen pounds of tallow per animal. His journals are filled with pages of information about wool grades, sheep crosses, and the number of employees in different aspects of the industry. For example, at the Rio Grande Estancia, a day's ride from Najmishk, 163 men worked at the canning factory, including tinsmiths, butchers, boners, preservers, mechanics, coopers, "grease men," skinners, and ear, and tail men. This didn't include all the men who worked on the farms, such as the shepherds, blacksmiths, cooks, and fencers.[24]

Furlong's iconic photographs present Najmishk as an enduring site of Selk'nam tradition, a form of ethnographic wonder. The second photograph in figure 4.7 reveals the stark omissions of this perspective. In the foreground stand several Selk'nam men wearing guanaco capes. They are ringed by a looming group of men on horseback. When I first saw this photograph, I feared it portrayed a group of bounty hunters or a military posse. Yet Furlong's caption reveals that this photograph is of a work crew on the Viamonte estancia. In his memoir, Lucas Bridges says he established Viamonte, which included the Najmishk village within its boundaries, to provide the Selk'nam with protection. Two of the caped men in the photograph were Furlong's guides Puppup and Chalshoat. All the men on horseback, except for Lucas Bridges and his unnamed Argentine foreman, are Selk'nam shepherds and ranch hands. This photograph offers a glimpse of realism at a moment when reality was becoming radically transformed by loss. Najmishk was not just an ethnographic museum and a safe haven from the violence to the north; it was also a reservoir of captive labor.

4.7 On the left, Chalshoat is standing, while Puppup is flaking an arrow point, surrounded by their wives and children. The group sits in front of Chalshoat's camp, covered in guanaco hide. On the right, Lucas Bridges is second from the right, on horseback, with Aanikin on horseback immediately to the left. Except for an Argentine foreman to Bridges's right, all others are Selk'nam shepherds and ranch hands, including Puppup (*center, standing*) and Chalshoat (*standing on the right*). Both photographs were taken at Najmishk, January 1908.

RUNNING OUT OF FILM

Midway through Furlong's trip, he realized he needed more film. He had already taken hundreds of photographs of Fuegian people along the Beagle Channel and southern Tierra del Fuego, as well as of ships, shipwrecks, and glaciers along the way. Now, in the heart of Tierra del Fuego and Selk'nam territory (the landscape that he considered key to his legacy), he feared he was going to run out of film. This dread is rarely part of being an anthropologist today, though many of us remember that desperate feeling when all the film cartridges in your backpack were spent. Luckily, months earlier, Furlong had arranged to have some extra film delivered to Estancia Sara, on the northwest coast of Tierra del Fuego.[25]

When Furlong made the decision to retrieve the film, he and Aanikin were already at the Viamonte estancia, where Furlong was beginning to take his iconic images at Najmishk. Estancia Sara was a few days north of Viamonte by horseback, though getting there was dangerous as it required crossing the unpredictable Rio Grande. Furlong planned to ride to Estancia Rio Grande, about a day's trip away. From there, he was going to coordinate their river crossing. On the other side of the river was an Argentine government patrol station and jail. He hoped to convince one of the patrol agents to travel to Estancia Sara, another three-day ride, to retrieve his film.

His plan fell apart at the Estancia Rio Grande. Furlong's account is very detailed, but to summarize, the rapid rise of the river forced him to quickly cross the river and leave Aanikin behind. In his long and complicated story about getting film, he says the following about arriving at Estancia Rio Grande: "McClellan [sic], who is in charge, soon came down to meet me. . . . McClellan is the man who perhaps has the worst reputation for cruelty in killing of the Indians of any man in T.D.F. and it was with the greatest difficulty that I had induced Aanikin to accompany me."[26] Furlong is referring to Andrew MacLellan, also called "Red Pig," an adventurer hired by Jose Menéndez to manage the Estancia Rio Grande.[27] Furlong describes MacLellan as a "short, powerfully built man, of Scotch Canadian descent, [with] florid red cheeks, bull dog jaw, orange red hair, and green eyes, and one could see at a glance that there was no sentiment lost in his makeup."[28]

Furlong understood the risk Aanikin was taking in traveling beyond the safety of Viamonte. The Rio Grande, as I described in the prior section, was the dividing line between the violent north and the relative safety of southern Tierra del Fuego. He felt terrible about leaving Aanikin in this dangerous position, as he described in his journal: "I could not help regretting

4.8 Furlong's portrait of Aanikin (*left*). Andrew MacLellan, on the left, with the unnamed foreman of the estancia (*right*). On the back of the photograph, Furlong wrote that MacLellan "had the reputation of being one of the Onas' [Selk'nam's] bitterest enemies and was held responsible for having offered a bounty of a pound sterling a head for an Ona, the left ear being required as evidence."

that I had not brought Aanikin with me [to the patrol station], and felt no little concern for his welfare, for he was the first Ona who had been up to Rio Grande, probably, since the four who were recently shot down in their tracks, while on a peaceful mission to Rio Grande Estancia."[29]

Furlong left the patrol station before his film was delivered, as word reached the station's chief that someone had tried to kill Red Pig. Furlong rushed back, fearing that the would-be assassin was Aanikin. It wasn't. In any case, they decided to the return south, where it was safer for Aanikin.

Every time Furlong recounts this story, which he does several times in the archive, he emphasizes the river's danger and the stern warning he gave MacLellan to protect Aanikin. Still, the situation is hard to fathom. After returning home, Furlong painted Aanikin's portrait, which is now archived by the Smithsonian Institute. Furlong considered this portrait to be the best of his Fuegian work. Though not visible in the portrait, the Selk'nam genocide left their traces on Aanikin's body, including knife and bullet scars.[30]

Stolen Images

STOLEN IMAGES: CODA

In Punta Arenas, the mainland town in Chile that is the gateway to the archipelago, there are postcards for sale made from Furlong's and Gusinde's images of Fuegian peoples. In December 2018, I purchased a stack of these postcards, thinking I would compare them to Furlong's photographs when I got back to Dartmouth. Then, a week later, I mailed them home from the Chilean research station in Antarctica because I had no other postcards to send. That day I sat on the dusty floor in the station's upstairs meeting room, surrounded by groups of Chilean and US high school students, all part of a program I was helping to chaperone.[31] The flat midday sky, heavy with snow, pressed against the room's panoramic windows, and I was glad to be warm inside. All of us were quickly scribbling notes to family and friends, needing to finish before the imminent arrival of the Chilean postmaster, with her special Antarctica cancellation stamp.

It took three months for my postcards to show up in mailboxes in the United States. During that time the images lay dormant, concealed in canvas mail bags, before they traveled across Drake Passage in a Chilean military transport plane to Punta Arenas. From there, they slowly moved up Chile to Santiago, then dispersed to numerous distribution points in the United States. Tourists have been buying these Fuegian postcards for over a century, helping to instantiate a global circuit of lost tribes imagery that accounts, in part, for the enduring character of the World's End figure.

Even decades before the advent of digital technologies, it was difficult to maintain control over the reproductive life of photographs, particularly those charged with the refrains of loss and wonder. During his lifetime, Furlong struggled to curb the unauthorized replication of his photographs. He was indignant about this and included the following story in his archive to make this point: After his Fuegian expedition, he spent a couple of days in Punta Arenas, regrouping before embarking on the Patagonian leg of his trip. While there, he read his accumulated letters from home, repacked his gear, and ran various errands, including dropping off his last roll of undeveloped Eastman Kodak film for processing to Cándido Veiga, the only professional photographer in the city.[32] When Furlong returned to pick up his prints, Veiga told him that his film was actually blank. Veiga dramatically unfurled the blank roll to illustrate. Furlong left the studio dumbfounded and disappointed.

The issue became clearer a couple of years later when some tourist postcards from Punta Arenas arrived in his Massachusetts mailbox. Furlong

4.9 Postcard made from a stolen photograph taken by Charles Wellington Furlong. The postcard misidentifies the Yagán girls as "Onas."

immediately recognized the images as his own. A couple years later, he returned to Punta Arenas, this time as a lecturer on a cruise ship. Upon arrival, he and a well-connected lawyer confronted Veiga at his studio.[33] The men forced Veiga to return Furlong's negatives and destroy all the postcards made from the stolen images. Furlong was sure these measures ended the circulation of these stolen images. In his archive, he included what he thought were the only existing copies of the Veiga postcards. A century later, I purchased one of the Veiga postcards in Punta Arenas.

Even after writing this book, I am not sure if there is a way to contain the iconic photographs' reductive magic. Furlong's images of Fuegian peoples have become part of the loss-and-wonder vernacular that constitutes the Fuegian aesthetic and, more broadly, the figure of the World's End. Yet his less well-known images, those at the margins of the archive, help us see beyond these tropes. These images, blurry and poorly composed, document a settler landscape in the making: missions, sheep farms, sawmills, and frontier towns. At the time of Furlong's visit, the presence of the Argentine and Chilean states was barely discernable in the archipelago. Punta Arenas was "like a British colony," as one British clerk described it, where "English was spoken almost as much as Spanish." Commerce, including purchases at local stores, was negotiated in sterling.³⁴ The Bridges and other settler families spoke little Spanish. Their commercial, spiritual, and familial ties were directed toward England. In those days it was easier and safer to sail to the Falklands than through the channels and Strait of Magellan to Punta Arenas, the closest commercial center, and there was no overland route across Tierra del Fuego.

Thomas Bridges became aware of Argentina's claims in the region when four Argentine ships arrived in the Ushuaia harbor in 1883 to establish a subprefecture, sixteen years after he moved to his estancia. The process of staking this territorial claim was mundane, yet consequential: the Argentine flag was flown, followed by a twenty-one-gun salute. Yet the ritual's effects were devastating. In the wake of the boats' appearance in the harbor, Bridges says, measles spread rapidly through the Yagán communities. People died so fast "it was impossible to dig graves fast enough."³⁵ Very soon after, Chile and Argentina opened up the Fuegian frontier to other European, Chilean, and Argentine ranchers. This sequence of events occurred throughout the Americas.

If we look beyond the Fuegian aesthetic in Furlong's archive, we see the rapid instantiation of the colonial apparatus in Tierra del Fuego and other sites around the Beagle Channel. Furlong was there when Chilean and Argentine national claims were contingent and barely visible. His archive exposes the early stages of nation-making in the periphery. Yet over time his iconic photographs have become another mechanism of state inscription in the region. I learned this from José Herman, who lives in the Yagán community of Villa Ukika. Herman explained that Furlong's photographs, as well as the work of Gusinde and a few others, have frozen and consigned Yagán people to the past, transforming their lives and histories into a story of "national" heritage. The iconic images are like a temporal pause button.

The establishment of Furlong's archive at Dartmouth became the catalyst for the uncontrolled proliferation of his iconic images. Because he established his archive without any restrictions on the use of the materials, as was standard at the time, his images have spread with lighting speed, including among contemporary scholars. There are several expensive coffee-table books featuring Furlong's photography—books that no one in the Yagán community could afford. Alberto Serrano, who directs the Gusinde Museum on Isla Navarino, calls this scholarship "anti-collaboration." Paying attention to Furlong's stolen images has taught me that archives proliferate beyond the boundaries of their enclosure, like ghosts escaping a cemetery's walls.

Lewis Henry Morgan · *A Figure*

F7.1 Sketch of a beaver dam by Rudi Colloredo-Mansfeld.

In 2013, I gave a talk at the University of North Carolina on our research project about beavers in Tierra del Fuego. I ended the presentation by suggesting that we hesitate, with wonder, at the world-making capacities of beavers, even as we recognize losses to the Fuegian forests. Rudi Colloredo-Mansfeld, who was then chair of the Anthropology Department at UNC, suggested that there was something about beavers that was particularly conducive to wonder, probably their building capabilities. It was clear that Rudi had a special interest in beavers. After I got home, he sent me a lovely email that included several pages scanned from his personal journal. These included sketches of beaver dams near his parents' farm in Massachusetts. His journal notes offered thoughtful insights into beaver habits as well as the challenges of living with beavers.

Rudi is not the first anthropologist to be inspired by beavers. Lewis Henry Morgan, considered a father of American anthropology, wrote a curious and exhaustive book titled *The American Beaver and His Works* (1868). Today Morgan is mainly remembered for his theories of social evolution, kinship studies, and writings about the Iroquois. Professionally Morgan worked as a lawyer, living in Rochester, New York, where he served as a stockholder and director of a railroad company whose rail line connected inland iron ore deposits to ports in the Great Lakes. Though the line stretched only forty miles, it traversed a region that Morgan considered some of the last wilderness in the eastern United States.[1] While trout fishing in this area, he became fascinated by beavers, particularly their human-like industry. For the next decade, he embarked on a comprehensive and comparative study of beavers in the United States, including research trips to the Hudson Bay Territory, the Missouri River, and the Rocky Mountains.

If I talk to almost any anthropologist about my work on beavers, without hesitation the person will ask if I have read Morgan's work. Though I had glanced over the work, repeated suggestions that I consult the discipline's forefathers tends to have the opposite effect on me as a feminist scholar. In any case, most of us would prefer to eliminate much of nineteenth-century anthropology, including Morgan's *League of the Ho-de'-no-sau-nee, or Iroquois* (1851).[2] But then Robert Foster, an anthropologist at the University of Rochester, kindly invited me to give a talk on beaver anthropology as part of a series of events celebrating Morgan's two-hundredth birthday.[3] To honor the occasion, I abandoned my stubborn opposition to reading Morgan. As it turns out, *The American Beaver and His Works* is a beautiful and thorough examination of beaver life, whose scope and style follow some of the best naturalist traditions of the era.

It is clear that Morgan was absolutely fanatical about beaver industry. As a white capitalist investor and railroad developer, his appreciation is not too surprising. Yet he was not content for his book to serve as an encyclopedic account of beaver natural history; he wanted it to become a major intervention in the era's taxonomic conventions. In particular, Morgan was frustrated with zoology's practice of determining taxonomic difference solely on anatomical structure. As he said in the book's preface, "Each animal is endowed with a living, and, also, with a thinking principle, the manifestation of each of which are not less important and instructive than the mechanism of the material frames in which they reside. In a comparative sense, the former are intrinsically of higher concernment."[4] In other words, Morgan was interested in the intrinsic nature of beavers—their logics of living and thinking and feeling. His goal, it seems, was to write an anthropology of beavers that pushed the conventions of the natural sciences. At the same time, he understood the limitations of an anthropology of animals. The basic challenge, in Morgan's estimation, was that animals could not speak. Speaking with others is foundational to anthropological research. Indeed, throughout the text, Morgan refers to animals as "mutes." How can we know the interior worlds of animals when we cannot communicate with them?

Morgan's answer was to read the beaver's manipulations of the landscape, including their architectural creations, as evidence of their intrinsic nature. As he says, "There is no animal, below man, in the entire range of the mammalia, which offers to our investigation such a series of works, or presents such remarkable materials for the study and illustration of animal psychology."[5] Much of Morgan's book is dedicated to these works, with two chapters describing beaver dams and other chapters describing beaver canals, meadows, lodges, burrows, and trails. The text is illustrated with remarkable sketches of these structures and landscape features, which Morgan believed were material manifestations of the animal's interior life (their "psychology," "habits and properties," and "mental endowments").

For anthropologists who know Morgan's broader scholarship, it is not a stretch to say that he wanted to understand animals in ways comparable to his approach to studying human societies. For example, in *Ancient Society* (1877) he offers a materialist taxonomy of human societies largely based on their acquisition of technology and inventions—a methodology that seems astoundingly similar to his approach to beaver anthropology.[6] For Morgan enthusiasts, *The American Beaver and His Work* is rich with insights into his intellectual preoccupations, including kinship theory, his personal character, and the relationship of anthropology to animal studies.

For me, the book does something different. Morgan was clearly enraptured by beavers. He did not think that beavers were particularly smart, but he certainly admired and was intrigued by aspects of their nature that seemed human-like. This recognition of beaver-human trajectories of sameness and difference became the seed of his interest, perhaps even obsession. Because beavers cannot speak, Morgan read everything he could about the animals, corresponded with beaver experts, including scientists and hunters, and then dedicated all his free time, for several years, to the careful study of beaver habits. Through these immersions, he hoped to gain insight into the interior life of beavers. Still, Morgan felt uncertain in his conjectures. He referred to his unorthodox approach to beaver anthropology as "an experiment."[7] I would call it a practice of speculative wonder.

5 · DREAMWORLDS OF BEAVERS

5.1 Still from *Dreamworlds of Beavers* (2017), a film by Christy Gast, Laura Ogden, and Camila Marambio.

Dreamworlds of Beavers

One rarely sees a beaver,
As they spend their days hidden below tannin-dark waters.
They are fleeting.
Rows of chew marks in the bark of a fallen tree,
Castorium's oily residue,
Downed timber, draglines in the mud.

In the woods, beavers are graceless, lumbering.
Their ponds offer a lightness of being, a safe tranquility.
Light captures and enlivens microscopic particles.
The calm of a snow globe,
these sediments drift along the water column.

....

Beavers are night creatures.
Of course, they may not even notice the dark,
as they have such poor eyesight.
In a hazy blur, their world is enlivened by scent and sound.
Surely, beavers do not dream in images.
Instead their dreams offer an acrid, musty sensorium.
A vibrato of gnashing teeth.

A beaver's life acquires form in the water.
Over time, beavers evolved with land *and* water.
At some point, they learned forestry.
Later, they learned to build underwater dens.
We all make spaces that comfort us.

....

Piles of rough timber, tree limbs:
really, this is an architecture of kinship.
Kinship resists the logic of trees;
It is a much messier entanglement of relations.
Like other forms of domestic life,
the beaver's world comes into being through routinized labor.

Chewing and dragging, chewing and dragging.
Such repetition.

....

Silt, decades old, hovers and skips along every surface,
like the landscape of the moon.
For astronauts, water signals life's possibility,
though this seems a low bar for encountering the magic of other worlds.
Beavers practice this sort of magic.
Let us resist the indications of industry. "Busy as a beaver."
Instead, contemplate the intimacy of water.

THE FORCE OF THINGS BARELY SEEN

In Tierra del Fuego there are signs of beaver everywhere. Gnawed stumps and radiating networks of dead and dying trees trace the animals' advance across the landscapes. Still, you rarely see a beaver. In all the days and nights we spent looking for beavers in the archipelago, I saw a beaver only a few times.

In January 2013 our research collective went on a beaver sighting-seeing expedition with a tour group out of Ushuaia, an Argentine tourist town on the Beagle Channel. Lots of visitors come through Ushuaia on their way to Antarctica, so the streets are filled with expensive gear stores, cafés, and adventure travel tour operators. Our "beaver safari," as we jokingly called the expensive trip, included transport to Valle Hermoso (Beautiful Valley), a property about eighteen miles outside of Ushuaia, where a guide led us and a handful of international tourists through mucky peat bogs to a steep

5.2 Beaver traces in Tierra del Fuego, including footprints in the mud (*left*) and teeth marks on logs (*right*).

5.3 Camila Marambio examining a beaver scent mound, with gnawed tree stumps behind her. Photograph by Christy Gast.

riverbank. There we stood together in a frigid row, watching and photographing beavers swimming in the dark river below.

Andrés, our guide, felt that environmental concerns about beaver-related forest loss were unnecessarily sensational. In response, as dusk approached, he told sincere stories about the beaver families living along the river. We stood listening as evening softened the stark landscape of dead and dying trees that seemed to go on forever. Technically, these were "wild" beavers, just conveniently living on the land of a resourceful family who charged tourists to see them. It was a pleasant experience, since Andrés provided little cups of hot mulled wine while we stood at the river's edge in the cold rain. This beaver sighting was like saying you have visited a country but really only changed planes at the airport.

The year before, I saw a beaver's head briefly emerge in the middle of a giant pond on a ranch in the interior of Isla Grande in Chile. The pond had multiple lodges in it, suggesting that an extended family of beavers claimed this space. Though we stood around for another hour, the beaver never reappeared. As we waited and waited and waited, and night grew near, I worried that Derek and Giorgia thought I imagined the whole thing.

A few days later Derek collected a beaver from a creek along a dirt road within Karukinka Nature Park. At the time, Derek was a PhD student studying the fertility of introduced beavers. He did have a .22 rifle, which he used to collect his specimens, as killing is called in these contexts. I have some photographs of this animal, taken when she was lashed to the front grille of our Toyota pickup truck. In the photographs, her fur is wet and matted and her orangish teeth protrude at a bad angle. She looks so undignified in the images, I now regret taking the pictures. Later, after Derek removed her ovaries for analysis, Giorgia cooked the remainder of her for our dinner. Giorgia used a wide metal disk as a pan, probably a discarded tractor blade, which she carefully balanced over an open fire.

Derek, Giorgia, and I spent six weeks together, driving across the island's broad and windy grasslands (the pampas).[1] Here the landscape is dry and littered with the afterlife of sheep—old bones, tufts of fur, and dried-out dung. We often saw condors soaring high above, also drawn to this sheep landscape. Together the three of us traveled from one ranch to the next. At the estancias, I interviewed ranch hands and owners, trying to make sense of the landscape and the life of beavers on the pampas. It was always cold, which helped with the long weeks together without showers. Each estancia was about a day's drive apart. We filled the space in between by singing along to Led Zeppelin and other rock bands on the radio. I learned an enormous amount from Derek and Giorgia about life in southernmost Chile, and the fieldwork would not have been possible without their help.

While I was interested in talking to estancia people about beavers, Derek needed to collect more specimens for his dissertation project. Once, around the middle of November 2011, we showed up at an estancia around midday. The owner was not expected back until the next day, so we had some extra time on our hands. For a while, we hung out in the ranch house kitchen, where one of the few women I ever saw on the estancias was making homemade rhubarb jam and cooking mutton stew. I think she was married to the foreman.

Later that afternoon, Derek wanted to look for beaver lodges on some rivers several miles from the estancia's headquarters. As we drove, the terrain got increasingly rough and muddy. I expressed my concern a few times about our route, but Derek was confident. Needless to say, we got hopelessly bogged down, miles and miles from the warm rhubarb kitchen. We spent half the day trying every trick to get the truck liberated from the muck: engine revving, shoving, shoveling, various experiments with tire traction. I was mad at myself for not being a bit firmer, but I was always filled with doubt about how to read the landscape then.

That night the three of us slept in the front seat of the truck, upright and straddling the stick shift, needing each other's warmth against the Patagonian chill. I woke cramped and with a desperate need for a little space—the closeness of several weeks together had reached a tipping point. I was reminded of the way you can smile through a toddler's tantrums for several hours, until you reach a moment when all you can do is close yourself up in the bathroom, sit on the toilet, and will the door to stay closed. That is how I was feeling.

At daybreak we began our walk back to the estancia. We walked in single file for several miles, silent and exhausted. An hour in, I heard the sound of a snipe overhead. These birds are hard to spot on land, as they blend into the gray-green grasslands. For some reason, probably joy, they fly high into the sky, well out of sight. Then, rapid and zigzaggy, they dive down, almost to the earth. In the process, they do something with their wings, I don't know what, but it makes an eerie drumming sound.

We all stood together, peering up, listening to the soaring snipes. I reached into my backpack and found some granola bars. We walked on together, more amicably, and continued our search for beavers and beaver people.

PERFORMING BEAVER, WRITTEN WITH CHRISTY GAST AND CAMILA MARAMBIO

As feminist artists and filmmakers, my collaborators Christy Gast and Camila Marambio have pushed me to explore other modes of investigation, including performance. Christy is a New York–based sculptor, performance artist, and filmmaker, with an award-winning history of site-based projects that problematize the gendering and heteronormativity of nature. Camila is a Chilean curator, filmmaker, and performance artist, whose work has redefined curatorial practice while also making important contributions to posthumanist thinking. Though I have known Christy for a very long time, we began our collaboration as part of Ensayos, an interdisciplinary art and science research collective that Camila initiated in 2011. Ensayos, which in English evokes the idea of inquiry and the essay, is a nomadic, interdisciplinary residency program in Tierra del Fuego.

Christy and Camila bring a joyful experimentation to their practice, guided by an interest in what they have called "undisciplined research."[2] In one sense, undisciplined research is shaped by a "Let's see what happens" approach, directed at an open-ended question. In this case, the question was *How do we include beavers into the decision-making about their own future in Tierra del Fuego?* Simultaneously, the collaborative's commitment to understanding and participating in each other's research practices, ranging from field biology and philosophy to performance art, contributes to Ensayo's undisciplined culture as well. Christy and Camila have described the outcome of these collaborations: "Disciplines begin to unravel as we seek new approaches to ecological and social questions that have a global resonance. By devising new rules of conduct, an ethical system emerges from a reflection on how, within our different disciplines, we come to know what we know, and how this knowledge is communicated and comes to bear on the world."[3]

In different iterations, Ensayos collaborators have come together to understand several distinct aspects of the region's political ecology.[4] The first major Ensayos project was focused on invasive beavers, hosted by Karukinka Nature Park, a protected area managed by the Wildlife Conservation Society. As part of the Ensayos beaver project, we traveled to the Fuegian Archipelago several times between 2011 and 2014. In the process, we conducted fieldwork documenting the presence of beavers on the landscape, as well as efforts to control beavers in protected areas. We worked together in more traditional ethnographic research modes, such as participating in community meetings and in interviews with scientists, environmentalists, and other community members. We have also collaborated on films, lectures, essays, performances, and installations, including a two-week residency at the Kadist Art Foundation in Paris.

Working with Christy and Camila, I have learned to stay with their processes of investigation, which include site-based performances, though it has taken me years to appreciate the value of undisciplined research. Of course, Christy and Camila are both well-regarded scholars and artists, working within communities of practice where the ephemeral nature of performance and performance art is recognized and celebrated. This is not the case in my own academic community, anthropology, which mainly values publications and grants as career milestones. There are usually moments of tension within interdisciplinary collaborations, and it takes time, self-reflection, and trust to make them successful. In our collaboration, at least in the beginning, I was sometimes frustrated by the mismatch in our different expectations about what kinds of work is valued (by ourselves and by our disciplines). Particularly during performance-based experiments, I struggled with the feeling that I was "wasting" time, or that time spent "seeing what happens" was a form of work that could never translate into nything legible as anthropology, even though "hanging out" is a cornerstone of ethnographic research.⁵

This feeling that we were wasting time was exactly how I felt when Christy told me she was building two human-size beaver costumes and that she was bringing them to Tierra del Fuego for our next trip. At her core, Christy is a sculptor and textile artist and always brings this attention to materiality and craft to her feminist performance practice. She also knows me like a sister and realizes that I may be the least likely person on earth to wear a beaver costume in public (and, sadly, I have yet to do so). Even Camila, who is exceedingly comfortable in being uncomfortable, reacted with some surprise and a little dismay at Christy's beaver costume news. Camila thought, "Holy shit, Christy. We've been working so hard to have the scientist take us seriously, you're kidding me!" But Christy, being wise and trusting in the tenets of undisciplined research, had faith that if she brought the costumes to Tierra del Fuego, she would "figure out what to do with them."

The beaver costumes are wearable sculptures made from burlap, velvet, and other textiles. They are roomy enough so that almost anyone can wear them, and many people have worn them, from schoolchildren in Isla Navarino to Bruno Latour, a well-known French philosopher. Christy's first design criterion was that the costumes had to be collapsible so they could fit into a backpack. These costumes were always meant to travel—through multiple airports and the Fuegian forests and to galleries and other exhibition spaces around the world. The headpiece, which appears helmet-solid, also can be folded and was designed so that any handy material, such as newspaper or forest moss, could be used to pop out the beaver's face and mouth. Christy's main aesthetic inspiration was a lovingly worn Punch and Judy monkey puppet that she got in London decades ago. This helps to explain why these human-size beavers are actually very sweet rather than terrifying.

To my surprise and gratification, Christy and Camila's beaver performances have been foundational to my thoughts on wonder. As a body of work, these pieces demonstrate how performance can provoke curiosity about other worlds and other futures. In this case, Christy and Camila's beaver performances have catalyzed new ways of thinking and feeling about beaver worlds in the Fuegian Archipelago—for me and others. I will describe a couple of the key performance events in this body of work, then describe how this work opens up wonder. I have little background in performance studies. Instead I have paid attention to these performances as an ethnographer would: by listening closely to what is said (and what is not

5.4 Camila Marambio wearing the beaver costume, Omora Ethnobotanical Park. Photograph by Christy Gast.

said), as well as paying attention to how these events are received and enacted in different places, times, and communities.

While Christy and Camila have produced several performances and films that feature the beaver costumes, including a particularly beautiful film of a beaver driving a wooden motorboat through the canals of Venice, I am going to describe three works that illustrate the ways their performances have helped me think about wonder. These pieces are a performance and film entitled *Asunto Castor* (2014), which was developed for a Chilean theater festival; a film titled *Beaver Dance* (2014); and a film titled *Castorera (A Love Story)* (2014).[6]

THE BEAVER PROBLEM

Christy and Camila first debuted the beaver costumes at a public performance of *Asunto Castor* at the Museo Antropológico Martin Gusinde on Isla Navarino. This anthropology museum is one of the only public venues on

Dreamworlds of Beavers

5.5 *Asunto Castor* (2014) performance at the Museo Antropológico Martin Gusinde. Image shows visitors posing in the costumes while Camila takes their photograph.

the island, aside from the elementary school, and it is popular with both locals and tourists.[7] *Asunto Castor*, which roughly translates as "the beaver problem," began like an artist's lecture at a museum. Camila introduced Ensayos and the beaver project to a group of fifty or so community members, tourists, and staff and scientists from the nearby Omora Ethnobiological Park. Later she invited the audience to take a look at the taxidermy beaver on display in the next room. There the audience encountered Christy wearing the beaver costume. In a beaver-ish way, she was rearranging the museum's furniture. The audience was invited to interact and talk with the beaver. Later, audience members took turns wearing the beaver costume, asking each other questions (as beavers), and posing for pictures with the costumes.

Several years prior to creating the beaver costumes, Christy began making oversized textile-based sculptures of beaver tails. In a conversation, she described what led her to begin making beaver sculptures. In 2011 on her first trip to Tierra del Fuego, she was taking lots of photographs, with the intention of using the images later as source material for sculptures. In a former agricultural building at Lago Blanco, she shot a photograph that showed a row of beaver tails hanging from the rafter. Christy was really confounded and troubled by the image. She couldn't figure out why the trappers kept and displayed the tails. Were they trophies? Were the trappers going to use them for something later?

At her studio in Miami, she approached her sense of unease by reproducing the tails in the image using fabric, but—importantly—she remade the tails to be "monumental." At this increased scale, the tail sculptures were now more proportionate to a human body than a beaver body. For Christy, the process of blowing up the object is a form of critical translation, or a way of magnifying "this thing that was kind of insignificant into something monumental." Christy's human-size beaver costumes focus attention in similar ways, which is particularly important since beavers (as living animals) are rarely seen in Tierra del Fuego.

More broadly, the beaver costumes enable participation in a thought experiment, or a speculative practice that unsettles or suspends reality, even briefly. Philosophers construct thought experiments by stripping complex ethical issues down to their key variables. This process, as Julian Baggini employs in his book *The Pig That Wants to Be Eaten*, helps control the contingencies that make ethical reasoning difficult in real life. In doing so, thought experiments help clarify the fundamental aspects of difficult ethical problems (such as eating meat). The ethical complexities of attending to invasive beavers in Chile are equally knotty (from debates about beaver agency to monetary evaluations of forest loss). In all these debates and discussions, beavers are largely "invisible in the conversation about their future," as Christy explained.

After getting over the initial awkwardness of being confronted by a human-size beaver, the audience at the museum engaged in this beaver thought experiment. As Camila suggests, "When you take the risk of opening the forum and allowing the public to participate, it is highly probable that the first fifteen minutes will be very uncomfortable." Christy's and Camila's experience has taught them that these periods of awkward silence do end *and* eventually lead to something novel, unforeseen, and transformative. In the museum, after the awkward period passed, the audience began to playfully interact with the beavers. Some audience members put on the costumes and answered questions from the standpoint of the beaver. For some, the experience of performing beaver revealed the limitations of their knowledge about these animals. Christy recalled that a lot of answers to questions were "I don't know" or "I don't know how they feel."

The audience's doubts ("Should I answer as a man or a male beaver?") reveal glimmers of cross-species curiosity. Watching the video of the performance, it is clear that humor and play are important catalysts of this curiosity. For example, after the performance was over, the audience lined up to have their picture taken in the beaver costume, like visitors to a Disney theme park. Playful curiosity is an affective register typically absent in discussions about invasive species and their killability. For many in the audience, the thought experiment ("What is it like to wear the body of a beaver?") provoked curiosity about beaver practices of living and dying in the archipelago beyond the parameters of their environmental impacts. This is the only time I have seen a public discussion about beavers in Tierra del Fuego where this has happened.

BEAVER SENSORIUMS

To prepare for the *Asunto Castor* performance, Christy and Camila practiced wearing the beaver costumes in the forests of the Omora Ethnobotanical Park. Christy described needing to spend time in beaver-impacted landscapes prior to the performance. She thought of this preparation as a way of "helping us to have empathy for the beavers, or think like them, or just move through the space in a different way." During this time, Christy and Camila filmed themselves negotiating the landscape wearing the costumes.

Christy designed the costumes specifically to explore the ways beavers sense the world.[8] The costumes function as beaver sensoriums. For example, she used burlap to cover the eyes of the headpiece, which mimics the limited eyesight of beavers. Beavers are clumsy on land, their bodies more adapted to the buoyancy of water. I have watched the raw footage of Christy and Camila moving around the Omora forests while wearing the beaver costumes; these usually graceful women seem to trudge through the forest, their bulk slowing everything down. They stumble over their large tails. The forests' thick network of branches and fallen limbs seem an insurmountable tangle.

That said, neither Christy or Camila was "pretending to be a beaver." Instead, as Camila explains, she felt somewhere in between, as if she was "inhabiting an alien space, which is not me and not beaver." Rather than being a beaver, in some ways the costumes heightened her awareness of being human. As she moved clumsily through the landscape, vision obstructed, dragging a heavy tail, Camila could not help but compare how she inhabits her own body in relation to how beavers live in the world. Wearing the costumes forced her to recognize how much she relies on her sight and agility, and even her hands and fingers, to navigate space. Wearing the costumes became a performative strategy that allowed her to grasp the sensorial trajectory that divides humans and beavers. In some ways, the costumes mask or muddle all the identities and abilities of being human, becoming an exercise of embodied difference. Performing beaver, in this context, became a way of exploring the affective registers that compose and differentiate beaver and human worlds.

Both Christy and Camila also noticed that moving through the forest, slow and clumsy, made them more attuned to trees. They described this as an unexpected attentiveness to trees, which was the direct result of wearing the costumes. For Camila, this moment of insight came when she grabbed a tree branch as she was about to fall over. In the process, she really noticed the tree's architecture and thought, "Beavers' relationship with trees must be so much more complex than I understand. Beyond function and form, I think they have co-evolved in ways that must include desire.... That illuminating thought wasn't a scientific revelation (because this is something evolutionary biologists have written about), but it was an incarnated knowing, something I came to know by feeling it in my body at that very moment." Christy too noticed that she was paying attention to trees in new ways that spoke to desire—tree desire, in this case. I was really struck by what they learned about beaver-tree relationships. In general, we tend to conceive of beavers' interactions with trees as work, labor, or industry. Beavers are described as architects, engineers, and even masons. After talking to Christy and Camila, I began to think of beavers as tree-desiring animals instead.

My favorite outcome of Christy and Camila's experimentation with the costumes is the short film *Beaver Dance*. In the piece, Christy and Camila dance on a wooden platform, which juts out over a creek in the Omora Ethnobotanical Park. The platform feels like a stage, while the forest beyond provides a natural and verdant backdrop. There is something strangely absorbing and beautiful in the graceful movements of these oversize beavers—like a scene stolen from a David Lynch film.

On several occasions, we have projected *Beaver Dance* on a screen as a backdrop while people enter a room for a talk, performance, or presentation. Rather than using the ambient forest sounds, we have overlaid the scene with random pop music. As Christy says, "It's kind of absurd and it's also very beautiful and slow. So people come in and no matter if they are expecting a talk by a scientist, or an artist talk, or a talk on ecopolitics and

5.6 Still from *Beaver Dance* (2014).

philosophy, nobody is expecting to see beavers dancing to Beyoncé." For the audience, *Beaver Dance* is a bit inscrutable. Is it supposed to be funny? Serious art? Bad art? This inscrutability helps cleanse the space of preconceived ideas and, like any good thought experiment, opens up the possibility of new ways of thinking.

A BEAVER LOVE STORY

Of course, not everyone is open to how performance can shift thinking and provoke curiosity. During the *Asunto Castor* performance at the Museo Antropológico Martin Gusinde, an ornithologist in the audience kept trying to bring the conversation back to the devastating environmental impacts of beavers on native habits and species. As I watched him speak, I imagined his words as a kind of net cast out to capture and rein in the parameters of engaging with the "beaver problem." I also felt enormous sympathy for his desire to control the discussion, as he reminded the audience of the real ways in which forest loss is impacting the rare and spectacular Magellanic woodpecker.

Scientific training and culture instill particularly rigid boundaries on what counts as knowledge and on the methods of gaining knowledge. Or, as Camila explained, "The difference between Art and Science is that in the Arts we know, trust, and invest in the value of playing with the ridiculous. Out of bounds. Out of our minds." I thought about this cultural divide

5.7 Production still from *Castorera (A Love Story)* (2014).

when I was talking with Christy and Camila about their 2014 film *Castorera (A Love Story)*.

In this film, Derek and Giorgia, my fieldwork assistants on my first research trip, wear the beaver costumes while engaging in the regular routines of their life, like chopping wood for the stove, eating, brushing their teeth, and snuggling together in their bed. Camila filmed this performance at Derek and Giorgia's *parcela*, a term for a rural quasi-farm property. In making the film, Camila gave Derek and Giorgia little direction, except to suggest that they remain a bit attuned to "beaverness" as they went about their daily activities. The resulting film is a thoughtful provocation on multispecies practices of kinship and domesticity.

When I heard about Derek and Giorgia's participation in this project, I was a little surprised. At the time, they were passionately concerned about the environmental impacts of beavers on the Fuegian environment. They are also serious and well-respected scientists. That said, they are both very open-minded and adventurous people, and so they agreed to become "anthropomorphic beavers," in Derek's terms, because it seemed like fun.

In addition to being fun, their collaboration on the film and other Ensayos performance are thought experiments. For example, Giorgia told me that the performances helped her think about beavers as "creative and feeling beings" rather than just problems to be solved. Derek echoed Giorgia's perspective, saying that the Ensayos collaborations gave him an opportunity to "open up and be curious." For Derek, the performances were particularly freeing since they were undertaken without the pressure of a preordained outcome (like an academic journal article).

In the field, Derek and Giorgia are keen observers of beaver natural history. When we were working together, they often pointed out specific plants and flowers that beavers like, such as *cadillo*, a pink-flowered perennial herb. From them, I learned numerous things about beaver inscription practices, including how to recognize beaver tracks, scat, slides, and pathways in the forest. In the film, they seem to channel what they know about beaver inclinations in their performance. For example, they spend a lot of time cutting and hauling wood that is used in the parcela's stove for heating and cooking.

Watching the film, I can't help but compare and contrast the domestic lives of beavers and humans. Watching these human-size beavers go about their domestic tasks reminds me of the repetition and routinization of domestic life for both beavers and humans. If my kitchen had a forest floor, the grass would be trodden in pathways linking the sink, stove, and fridge.

Christy and Camila recognize the power (and even magic, in Camila's description) of the costumes to dislodge preconceptions and provoke curiosity about other species, even if it means recognizing the limitations of what we can know and feel about their worlds. In the beginning of our collaboration, I was not convinced that their performance work had any bearing on my own work as an anthropologist and theorist of multispecies relations. As it turns out, their performance work has been critical to the ways I conceptualize wonder as a practice of curiosity. I am grateful that they have patiently kept me in their web of undisciplined research.

Traces of Derrida · *A Figure*

F8.1
Laura Balance, from the band Superchunk, is on the left, while I am (I think) on the right. Photograph by Bill Bryson, 1992.

Traces of Derrida can be found throughout this book. Though he is largely unwelcome, I am unsure how to write a book about archives and history without acknowledging his presence. I first read Derrida in graduate school, over twenty years ago now. During that time, I worked a few nights a week as a bartender at an indie rock club in downtown Gainesville, Florida. Perhaps because of this, the soundtrack of early 1990s punk bands enliven my memories of poststructuralist theory. After closing, we would mop up the spilled beer, scrub down the sticky counters, and haul the trash to the dumpster. Later, in the silence of the cool night, I would ride my bike home, the smell of cigarette smoke and disinfectant lingering in my wake. Derrida lingers in the same way.

I moved to Gainesville for graduate school in 1991. The year before, five college students were savagely tortured and killed by Danny Rolling, a serial murderer who targeted petite brunette women.[1] For years, television news programs showed images of body bags being hauled out of brick apartment buildings. In these serialized images, ashen-faced detectives stood around, avoiding the camera's gaze. During those years, simple acts, like riding a bike home at night, reminded me that I lived in a world both the same as and different from the men in my life. My world included repetitive door locking, hot nights sleeping with the windows shut, and other rituals to ward off becoming prey. During this time, my feminism became a deeply entrenched part of my being, though largely absent from my intellectual life.

Graduate programs in the 1990s were enamored with male, continental philosophy. Certainly we read women anthropologists, but generally in courses that were topically marked as appropriate to this kind of scholarship, such as courses on "women and gender" or "the Caribbean." Coco Fusco, now a professor of art at Cooper Union, recently described the sexual politics of "theory" in this era as well as her sexual assault by the ethnographic filmmaker Jean Rouch.[2] In Fusco's account, male continental philosophy, particularly Lacan and Derrida, served as the intellectual currency of the era's avant-garde and predatory art scene.

Male continental philosophy is what counted in my graduate program too. We were all enamored with Michel Foucault, Jacques Derrida, Roland Barthes, Walter Benjamin, and others, and sought recognition within this masculine star system. In my own work, Gilles Deleuze and Félix Guattari, in particular, opened up the liberating possibilities of other forms of ethnographic writing. I first read their work in graduate school, and then spent the next ten years thinking through their ideas, a process that culminated in my book *Swamplife*. What you learn in graduate school becomes part of your intellectual foundation (another form of archive). At times I am profoun[d]ly saddened by the absences within this intellectual archive, hence my a[mbi]guity about Derrida's presence in this book.³

For years, the photo at the beginning of this entry hung behind the bar at the *Covered Dish*, the club where I worked during graduate school. Even during those years, I barely recognized myself in the image. "It is probably me" should serve as the photo's caption. Sometimes a photograph will capture a facial expression that other people recognize as you, even when you are unsure. This photograph, I believe, stilled my face as I turned toward Laura Balance, freezing an angle I had never seen before. To this day, I dislike the way the skin above my eyes droops in photographs. Other memories, now also hazy, confirm my identity in the photograph. Laura Balance and I had been friends and neighbors as undergraduates in Chapel Hill, North Carolina. Still, other people think it is a picture of the musician Shannon Wright. Derrida would have called this Polaroid an archive, or a gathering of signs that are simultaneously remembered and forgotten. This is the nature of the "trace."

In this book I would like to move beyond uncertainties of the Derridean trace. Instead, let us consider the affective register of the archive as another kind of truth, in this case, the intimacy of friends and how "theory" can silence ways of knowing the world—ways of knowing that linger like a trail of cigarette smoke.

Anne Chapman · *A Figure*

F9.1 From Ondinnok's performance of *A World That Comes to an End—Lola*, directed by Yves Sioui Durand and choreographed by Leticia Vera. This scene shows Anne Chapman listening as Lola Kiepja describes the origins of time, with Angela Loij translating. Photograph by Martine Doyon.

Anne Chapman was an American-born anthropologist who, in middle age, embarked on a new research project in some very remote regions of the Fuegian Archipelago. (As I did.) Chapman studied or worked with some of the most famous figures in anthropological history: Paul Kirchoff, Sol Tax, Karl Polanyi. Claude Lévi-Strauss was her mentor and supervisor for most of her professional career.[1] She admired her teachers, particularly Polanyi, who taught her to be critical of universal assumptions about human nature.

Reflecting on her career, she once wrote, "I may add here while all my professors were men, many of my informants were women." Except for colleagues and collaborators in Tierra del Fuego, I have rarely met an anthropologist who has heard of Anne Chapman, even though she published widely in multiple languages, made ethnographic films, and rigorously engaged with the key ideas of her time.[2] Most of us learn very little about the work of women anthropologists of my grandmother's generation, even though the ideas of her professors and colleagues are still taught. This portrait is a form of speculative feminism, to borrow a phrase from Donna Haraway, or an attempt to refigure anthropology.[3]

Chapman flew from Tegucigalpa to Punta Arenas in the fall of 1964, after Lévi-Strauss gave her permission to interrupt her ongoing fieldwork in Honduras. She and a small party then rode horses across Tierra del Fuego to meet Lola Kiepja, who was living on the Selk'nam reserve in Argentina. Kiepja, one of the last speakers of the Selk'nam language, was also a respected *xo'on*, a term that is often translated as "shaman."

Chapman said Kiepja became the "inspiration for all that followed." Here is how Chapman described Kiepja: "Lola impressed by her spontaneous laughter and her penetrating expression. She was not vanquished by the overwhelming tragedies of her life: her twelve children had passed away, mainly from imported diseases, her people and her culture no longer existed. She was alone, except for occasional visits of Garibaldi and the farm worker who brought her firewood, matches, meat and herb tea."[4]

Chapman's anthropology in Tierra del Fuego has been rightly criticized for its "salvage" rhetoric and inclinations, as well as her tendency to collapse Selk'nam culture into prehistory.[5] We should not ignore the ways she establishes her authority through these vernaculars of loss. Still, she dedicated her life to telling stories that she could barely comprehend, even as they urgently needed to be told. In 1966, when Chapman began her research in earnest, there were only thirteen people who identified as Selk'nam living in their homelands, all over the age of fifty.[6] In her conversations with Chapman, Kiepia gave accounts of lives lost to professional bounty hunters and lice raids. She witnessed trucks filled with dead bodies, all victims of the devastating measles epidemic of 1924–25.[7]

Kiepja was about ninety when she worked with Chapman, and she probably was the last Selk'nam person who recalled life before the genocide. In the months before Kiepja died, they worked nonstop, recording Selk'nam history, kinship terms, chants, and myths. Kiepja taught Chapman to speak Selk'nam, as well as the language of local birds and guanaco.[8] In Chapman's account, the small details are dear. For example, she says Kiepja was not very neat and was fond of wearing a man's ragged suit jacket. She "ate butter as if it were candy" and enjoyed an aperitif of sweet vermouth before dinner.[9] She liked to record and then listen to Selk'nam songs and chants. When it was very cold, she insisted they warm the tape recorders' batteries on the stove. Kiepja died during a freezing cold winter, months after Chapman returned home to Paris.

Selk'nam descendants who survived the genocide scattered to cities outside the region, though there remains a small community at Rio Douglas in Argentina. At the height of the genocide, Selk'nam survivors were forcibly relocated to missions, such as the one on Isla Dawson, where some children were adopted out or sent to live in cities as servants. The scattered and urban Selk'nam became largely invisible to the Chilean state and to anthropologists, as they no longer conformed to settler expectations of being Indigenous. Also, being Indigenous was not safe.

Yanten Gomez, who goes by the name Keyuk, grew up in Santiago. His mother, Ivonne Gomez Castro, was wary of telling her children about their Selk'nam heritage, according to the journalist Judith Thurman.[10] Still, Keyuk, an autodidact who studied linguistics, taught himself Selk'nam while still in his teens. He now composes songs in Selk'nam, performing them in an "ethno-electronic" band, and produces Selk'nam language video guides. He learned the language, in part, by listening to Chapman's recordings of Lola Kiepja. It seems, in another articulation of entangled time, Kiepja is no longer the last Selk'nam speaker.[11]

CONCLUSION · Birdsong

C.1 Furlong described the Darwin's rhea in this photograph as a "dancing tame ostrich." The bird seems framed by a halo of light.

My field notes are filled with observations about birds, a habit I picked up from my ornithologist father. When I travel to places that feel like nature, as surely Tierra del Fuego does, there are always moments when I realize that my father's bird wonder is edging out my duties as an anthropologist. For example, during the second week of November 2011, I was so thrilled by the lesser rhea (*Rhea pennata*), a small ostrich-type bird, that I recorded little else about my visit to the Patagonian mainland. Instead of ethnographic observations, my field notes carefully catalog how the rheas dart and flutter across the steppe, with "crazy, dodgy, jerky, leapy movements." These are flightless birds, yet when spooked they spread their wings wide and speed across the grasslands "like an airplane too heavy to take off," or so my notes describe them. Male rheas spend forty days incubating the eggs of multiple females, a reversal of things that I found particularly compelling. Bird lovers know that the lesser rhea enchanted Darwin as well. Darwin's rhea, as they are also called, was a catalyst to his curiosity about the origin and difference of species.[1]

But loss can extinguish wonder about other worlds, as I also discovered in Tierra del Fuego. Within two months of my return to the United States from my first research trip to the archipelago, my father became very ill and died. I have few words to describe his death except to say that when I returned to the islands a few months later, Tierra del Fuego had changed in my absence. It was as if an ambivalent haze had cloaked the landscape. I could not bear to even think about birds. I could not scribble lists in my bird guides. Andean condors, surely one of the world's most wonderous birds, filled me with rage.

Grief can calcify our curiosity about other worlds. In many communities, grief over loss (habitat, species, territory, language), or at least the threat of loss, determines the ways care is extended to other lives or is withheld. Yet loss and wonder are contingent refrains in compositions of the present. As affective formations, loss and wonder are not pure and untethered from politics and history; they emerge out of the apparatuses that make living and dying unjust and unequal modes of existence. Even so, in the forests of the Fuegian Archipelago, a landscape resonant with multiple histories of loss all more significant than my own, I learned to keep open the possibility of wonder. I learned this from listening to the sounds and silence of birds.

SILENT FORESTS

Isla Navarino's Omora Ethnobotanical Park focuses its environmental education efforts on the forest's small wonders. *Omora* is the Yagán word for hummingbird, the tiniest of birds. Under the leadership of Ricardo Rozzi, a Chilean environmental philosopher and ecologist, the park has developed programming it calls "ecotourism with a hand lens."[2] In this approach, students and visitors immerse themselves in the region's "miniature forests," which are composed of lichen, liverwort, and moss. In this way, the park offers a wilderness experience that counters tourist expectations of epic World's End's landscapes—such as glaciers, rugged mountains, or skies filled with Andean condors.

Not far from the entrance to the park, a trail winds through a well-marked garden of these small botanical specimens. Interpretive stations along the trail feature permanent lens-shaped metal rings that spotlight the miniature species, their habitats, and associated invertebrate fauna. On many occasions, I have come across visiting college students and cruise ship visitors peering through magnifying lenses at the carpeted forest floor or at lichen growing up trees. In contrast to much of the World's End tourism, Omora's miniature forest forces visitors to slow down, like mud, and notice worlds that are largely unknown and easily overlooked.

The pounding of Magellanic woodpeckers frequently intrudes upon the calm of Omora's miniature forests. These woodpeckers drum on any available wooden surface, from tree trunks to wooden handrails. Like other practices of inscription, their drumming is one way the birds stake territorial claims in the forest. Magellanic woodpeckers are enormous birds, quick and cartoonish, yet strong as jackhammers. Their long and sturdy bodies are shiny black, with a little white patch along their shoulder blades. The males look like their heads have been dipped in crimson paint. Birders come to the Fuegian forests to view these majestic birds, iconic species of southern Patagonia and also the closest surviving relative of the extinct ivory-billed. While the woodpecker has many admirable qualities, it is the bird's nearness to extinction that lures birders to visit these remote forests, including myself.

When Rachel Carson wrote *Silent Spring* in 1962, she and her editor understood that loss has an acoustic register. The original working title of Carson's manuscript, "Man against the Earth," reflected the urgency Carson felt about the dangers of chemical contaminants in the twentieth century, from chemical warfare to industrial agriculture.[3] Carson and her editor retitled her manuscript to capitalize on "silent spring's" affective power to spur scientists and environmentalists into action. A forest silenced of birdsong was so apocalyptic and simultaneously relatable, *Silent Spring* became the rallying cry for the environmental movement and the campaign to outlaw the pesticide DDT.[4] In the Fuegian Archipelago, the fear of a silent forest, in this case one devoid of spectacular woodpeckers, has become a key justification for forest conservation in the region.

Other forms of silence also leave their traces in Omora's forests. In addition to calling attention to overlooked botanical wonders, Omora's mission and educational materials also highlight overlooked forms of ecological knowledge.[5] Along the forest's trails, there are placards offering ethno-ecological interpretations of forest biota. These signs identify plant and animal species in four languages: Yagán, Spanish, English, and Latin. For the biosphere reserve managers this is a political act that goes beyond mere translation: these signs are forms of inscription that make ethical claims about the coexistence of multicultural forms of knowledge within the park's territory. Coupled with the park's educational programming and outreach to the Yagán community, these interpretive signs are important interventions into knowledge hierarchies and universal claims about science typically found within conservation efforts. But as I stood in the forest, reading the words on the signs, I realized that this way of inscribing Yagán presence in the forest also magnified other forms of loss. For example, there is only one fluent speaker of the Yagán language left in the world. Thus the interpretive signs' inscriptions of presence trace absence simultaneously.

WAX CYLINDERS

In the Furlong Papers are recordings of Fuegian men and women singing traditional songs in the Yagán and Selk'nam languages. Furlong made these recordings using an Edison phonograph machine, a big bulky instrument that recorded audio onto hard wax cylinders. At the time of Furlong's expedition, cylinder recorders were widely used by linguists and anthropologists concerned with the loss of Indigenous languages and culture. In marketing the machines, Thomas Edison stressed the recorders' importance as an unbiased technology for language preservation.[6] Always meant to be archival, these recorders were part of salvage anthropology's toolkit. From these cylinders I learned a lot about the nature of the trace, as well as the contingencies of loss and wonder.

When you consider the life of these fragile cylinders, their existence seems improbable. Over a hundred years ago, the Edison recorder, weighing over twenty pounds, was packed away in a trunk for Furlong's voyage from Boston to Punta Arenas. Then it was hauled by clipper ship down to the archipelago, where it was transported by horse and mule across Tierra del Fuego and on small boats across the Beagle Channel. Only one photograph exists that features the recorder, though the machine is not visible in the image. Instead, the photograph shows a Selk'nam guide dragging a horse through a deep and muddy bog. Furlong must have taken the photograph while on his own horse, as the image is at an odd angle and blurry. The caption explains that the horse is carrying the sewing-machine-size recorder as well as the expedition's precious wax cylinders.

Several years later, Furlong described traveling with the cylinders in a letter to Erich von Hornbostel, an Austrian ethnomusicologist who used this same technology to record Pawnee narratives in 1906.[7] Furlong wrote:

> As an incidental thing it might interest you to know that these records were all carried across the entire island of Tierra del Fuego from Beagle channel region to Porvenir in packs on pack horses. This involved the crossing of the Divide over the mountains, through bog lands in which my horses were bogged some times several times a day,—necessitating the removal of the packs in most cases,—passing through deep and almost impenetrable forest and at other times fording streams and even following stream beds in icy torrents for hours at a time. *It is a wonder that only two of these records were slightly cracked during the journey under what I consider the roughest traveling that will be found as a rule any where in the world.*[8]

Indeed it is a wonder that these cylinders survived the journey.

Furlong brought the Edison recorder to Tierra del Fuego intent upon archiving languages and cultures ravished by colonial expansion. His goal mirrors the technology's initial purpose, which was to capture sounds of life before they were silenced. Edison, in describing his invention's utility, suggested families could use it to record the last words of the dying.[9] Like the archive's dermatoglyphs, Furlong's wax cylinders offer a trace of life and existence, the voice, while simultaneously registering histories of loss and silence—the material embodiment of the Derridean trace if there ever was one. For Derrida the slippery articulation of absence and presence revealed the limitations of representation. Yet traces live in the world, accruing histories, memories, and erasures in the process. It matters how they touch us, as the touching has the potential to transform relations of living and dying in the present and the future.[10]

Over the decades, one of Furlong's cylinders cracked. Wax cylinders are very fragile, becoming brittle and hard with age. Dust and mold build up on their surfaces, distorting and muffling sound. Over time and repeated playing, the grooved inscriptions dull. All these problems plagued Furlong's recordings. Recognizing their precarity and importance, Peter Carini, an archivist at Dartmouth College, arranged to have the broken cylinder repaired and the entire collection transferred to a digital format. This was a difficult and expensive task, but because of Carini's efforts, we were able to share the recordings with members of the Yagán community in the winter of 2016.

To hear the recordings, community members interested in Yagán history and cultural preservation joined Christy, Camila, and myself in a small conference room in the village overlooking the Beagle Channel. Listening to sounds of Yagán songs, recorded on wax cylinders a century before, was eerie and difficult. The voices in the recordings were barely audible, as the cylinders' roaring static overwhelmed the traces of song. At times the recordings sounded like muffled wailing or screeches riding the wind. Yagán hunters were acute mimics of kelp geese and albatross, so some of the songs may have been in the language of birds anyway. Listening to the recordings was like scanning the horizon of a foggy sea searching for a missing boat.

As we listened, Abuela Cristina, the only remaining fluent speaker of the Yagán language, sat off to the side, keeping warm by the wood stove. Abuela Cristina has shouldered the burden of being the last fluent speaker since her sister-in-law died over a decade ago, a distinction no one wants to inherit. After the recordings ended, we did not ask her if she understood any of the songs. The presence of loss was too palpable. Instead we spoke of technical problems with the audio and the possibilities of "cleaning them up." Then a German tourist knocked on the door requesting a photo with the Abuela.

The cylinders record moments of wonder as well as loss. In January 1908, Furlong was camped with Aanikin and his wives along the shore of Lago Fagnano in Tierra del Fuego. They spent several days at the spot, resting and enjoying the glacial lake. Furlong spent a lazy afternoon, lying on the lake's shore, watching the clouds drift overhead. According to Furlong, this land was part of Aanikin's home territory. Being there seemed to deeply move Aanikin. In Furlong's words, "This was the only time, so far, that

C.2   The Fuegian woods, where Furlong played a recording of Tininisk's voice. Photograph taken the following morning.

I saw Aanikin show any semblance of emotion. But the sight of these old hunting grounds of his seemed to stir something within him."[11]

One night Aanikin asked Furlong to play the "mechina" so that his wives, Warkeeo and Otroshoal, could hear "the wonderful sound of Tininisk's voice."[12] Tininisk, whom Furlong described as a "magician" or "medicine man," was wise to the loss-and-wonder economy and charged an unhappy Furlong $2 for this recorded performance. Other descriptions in the archive suggests Tininisk was a leading member of Aanikin's territorial clan. Imagine the scene: Furlong and Aanikin's family, huddled around the Edison recorder, as the dark night became enlivened with the sound of Tininisk's voice. There would have been a campfire, as the nights are cold in the Fuegian summer.

This is not a silent forest. Shrill black-faced ibis often roost in the canopy, so Tininisk's voice would have mingled with birdsong and other forest sounds. Of course, the recording was a version of Tininisk's voice rendered in wax, so the sound must have been familiar and also strange. Still, I am struck by the loss-and-wonder contingencies of the scene. Tininisk's voice filling the forest with the sounds of a Selk'nam ceremonial chant. This chant, just for a moment, competed with the other forest inscription practices, such as the ibis's shrill cry. In doing so, Tininisk re-inscribed presence upon their "old hunting ground," now lost to Aanikin and Tininisk, both of whom lived in refuge on the Bridgeses' estancias. Of the night, Furlong recorded only the following in his journal: "They knew Tininisk and it was interesting to watch their expression as the unseen sound broke in weird chant out into these solitudes."

After listening to Tininisk, Aanikin allowed Furlong to record his own voice. In the field, Furlong or a helper would have used a hand crank to operate the recorder's spindle. The spindle held the wax cylinder in place. To record the voices onto this cylinder, a person sang or spoke into the machine's fluted recording horn. My grandfather, who was anachronistic even in his youth, used to carry one of these around instead of using a hearing aid. Soundwaves travel through this horn to reach a pressure-sensitive diaphragm. A cutting needle, attached to the diaphragm, then inscribed the voices onto the cylinders. While this seems fairly straightforward, the recording process remains stubbornly incomprehensible to me. The magic just gets in the way of my willingness to make sense of this technology. Instead I stay with the wonder generated by a process that archived Aanikin's voice on the surface of a small wax cylinder, carried across the world, now stored away in a little box in the library just a short walk from my office on campus.

In the Yagán community, there are several efforts to make the language relevant again, including teaching children Yagán words and traditions. These recordings are too rough to become a part of language-revitalization efforts. Instead they do something else. Listening to the past sparks connections and claims to places and histories deemed lost by others. The cylinders' indecipherable chants, sometimes mimicking the songs of birds, animate the present—just like Tininisk inscribed presence on his old hunting grounds a century ago. Rather than being testaments to loss, the recordings attune their listeners to the possibility of a different future. This is wonder.

Gratitude · *A Figuration*

I am so grateful to the all the beings and places in the Fuegian Archipelago that have shared their time and stories with me, enriching this book and my life in the process. In particular, I would like to thank Alberto Serrano, Christy Gast, Camila Marambio, Bárbara Saavedra, Francisco Filgueira, Claudia Gonzalez, Derek Corcoran, Giorgia Graells, Christopher Anderson, and Pat and Eva Kelly for sharing fieldwork, conversation, hiking, cooking, and thinking. I have tried to make their voices and ideas visible in this book. Staff at Dartmouth College's Rauner Special Collections Library, particularly the archivist Peter Carini, provided enormous research support for this project. In the uncertain hours before the coronavirus's impacts restricted access to our libraries, Jay Satterfield, head of Special Collections, Joshua Shaw, Special Collections technology coordinator, and Phyllis Gilbert, processing specialist, organized and made high-resolution copies of this book's archival images. Their kindness and professionalism cannot be overstated. I am grateful for the support Ricardo Rozzi and the staff at the Omora Ethnobotanical Park gave us during our fieldwork on Isla Navarino in the Fuegian summer of 2015.

Sienna Craig and Abby Neely read this entire manuscript, helping me to see what was (and wasn't) working. I am very grateful to Marcos Mendoza, Sarah Kelly, Dana Powell, Grant Gutierrez, Arturo Escobar, Marianne Lien, Anne Rademacher, Alberto Serrano, George Holmes, Manuel Prieto, and Zac Caple for reading and commenting on sections of the manuscript. Parts of this book were discussed in several workshops, including "UnCommons: A Sawyer Seminar," organized by Marisol de la Cadena and Mario Blaser in 2015 at UC-Davis, where Casper Bruun Jensen and Kregg Hetherington provided insightful comments. I am very grateful for the generous engagement with my work at the "Workshop on Animals and Anthropology," organized by Dale Jamieson at NYU, particularly reviewer comments by Nikhil Anand and Yuka Suzuki. More recently I received very helpful feedback on the book's introduction from participants of the Political Ecology Reading Group at the University of Oslo, including Marianne Lien, Christian Krohn Hansen, Knut Nustad, Sylvia Yanagisako, and Marit Melhuus. Sections of this manuscript were published in the journal *Environmental Humanities*, where Thom van Dooren, Jamie Lorimer, and Astrida Neimanis offered insightful editorial advice, as did two anonymous reviewers. Several passages of this book also appeared in "Saturate," a chapter in *Veer Ecology: A Companion for Environmental Thinking*, edited by Jeffrey Jerome Cohen and Lowell Duckert. Jeffrey and Lowell's creativity were catalysts for this book project. Over the past few years, I have presented this material at numerous colloquia and lectures, and I am so very grateful for those opportunities. I thank in particular Anne Rademacher, Rayna Rapp, Helena Hansen, and Amy Zhang for inviting me to present the 2017 Dorothy Nelkin Lecture at NYU.

SIENNA CRAIG: Writing is solitary and difficult. It is an immeasurable gift to have a friend and colleague, like Sienna, who cares deeply about writing and is a generous critic. Traces of her editorial insights can be found throughout this book. A few years ago, we started an ethnographic writing workshop at Dartmouth. The first year, we invited Katie Stewart and Paul Stoller to help lead the workshop on the ethnographic possibilities of loss and wonder. Their influence continues to shape our process and approach to ethnographic writing. From Katie we learned the value of reading our work out loud to each other. Those moments of shared vulnerability have transformed a group of writing colleagues into an extended writing family. We were honored that Bob Desjarlais and Marianne Lien led subsequent workshops on themes of care, voice, and audience. Bits of this book began at the workshop, five hundred words at a time, and I am grateful to my writing family for their gentle improvements: Ann Armbrecht, Dwai Banerjee, Sabrina Billings, Elizabeth Carpenter-Song, Grant Gutierrez, Maron Greenleaf, Tracey Heatherington, Sarah Kelly, Chelsey Kivland, Patricia Lopez, Abby Neely, Bernie Perley, Jesse Shipley, and Yana Stainova. I am also grateful to Dartmouth's president Phil Hanlon for supporting this effort.

PAIGE WEST: Several years ago, Paige began to encourage the Anthropology and Environment Society to reflect upon the gender inequalities of our citational practices and to think critically about who and what counts as "theory" within political ecology. I am exceedingly grateful to the community that the gender politics effort has produced, as well as what I have learned from them, particularly Molly Doane, Nicole Peterson, Bridget Guarasci, Jessica Cattelino, Amelia Moore, Sarah Vaughn, and Amy Zhang. Bridget, Amelia, and Sarah led the effort to produce the "Syllabus for a Progressive Environmental Anthropology," which has become a key resource for teachers and students. The commitments resulting from those conversations have been foundational to this book's structure and approach to theory.

Last, I am so grateful to Duke University Press. Alejandra Mejía, editorial associate, has patiently helped with endless technical questions, and Gisela Fosado, editorial director, has offered encouragement and intellectual guidance throughout the publication process, while Lisl Hampton has carefully stewarded this project through the important design and production stages. I am very grateful, as well, to the two anonymous scholars who reviewed this manuscript. Thank you all.

Notes

The World's End

1 Furlong, "The Alaculoofs and Yahgans, the World's Southernmost Inhabitants," 420.
2 For a history and discussion of glaciation in the Southern Patagonian Ice Field, see Lliboutry, "Glaciers of Chile and Argentina," 1108–1206.
3 The largest island in the archipelago is officially named Isla Grande de Tierra del Fuego. Throughout this manuscript, I use *Tierra del Fuego* to describe the largest island, as this is still commonly used, and it aligns with archival sources as well.
4 Ogden, *Swamplife*.
5 In this book, I use the term *apparatus* to describe a governing structure that seeks to capture or entrain other beings and things into its semio-material logics. As an example, in 1958 Zora Neale Hurston used the term to describe southern Florida's commercial agriculture system, saying, "It has evolved into a production machine, a device, an apparatus, an invention, under the supervision of both state and government." In her description of this agricultural apparatus, she importantly includes not only African American farm labor, state policy, infrastructure, and the economic system, but also southern Florida's rich muck soils and flowing rivers. See Hurston, "Florida's Migrant Farm Labor," 200. I am indebted to Jessica Cattelino for sharing Hurston's piece with me. See Abbott, "Recovering Zora Neale Hurston's Work," for historical context of this piece and Hurston's work more broadly. In addition, the philosopher Giorgio Agamben provides two helpful insights into the political characteristics of an apparatus: first, an apparatus strategically and concretely reinforces existing relations of power; second, within and through an apparatus, relations of power intersect with relations of knowledge. He goes on to say that an apparatus is "anything that has in some way the capacity to capture, orient, determine, intercept, model, control, or secure the gestures, behaviors, opinions, or discourses of

living beings." Agamben, "What Is an Apparatus?," 14. Settler colonialism, though uniquely configured in the Fuegian archipelago, is an apparatus.
6 Bridges, *Uttermost Part of the Earth*, 24.
7 In "Inventing Tropicality," David Arnold convincingly shows how the "tropics" were invented as a moral category that enabled centuries of European exploration and exploitation in the Southern Hemisphere. European ideas about tropical places and people became conceptually contingent, Arnold argues, with the heat-drenched excesses of the "jungle" becoming a metonym for the moral character of Indigenous peoples too. Something similar happens with European representations of polar peoples and landscapes. Both are ways of knowing and representing place that are imbued with European privilege and colonial logics. Both are ways of constructing place and people as alien and dangerous. Still, the affective resonances of the World's End are specific to ideas about life on earth's southernmost settlements, as I explore in this book. Simone Abram and Marianne Lien examine how "geopolitical and economic processes" produce political peripheries that are simultaneously bound up with contemporary ideas of wilderness ("Performing Nature at World's Ends," 5). Similarly, Paige West uses the term *representational rhetorics* to describe the way a bundle of images shapes how Papua New Guinea and its peoples are known and governed, as well as supports ongoing inequalities and practices of dispossession (*Dispossession and the Environment*, 5).

Introduction

Figure I.1 is from MSS-197, Box XI, Folder 26, Furlong Papers. Henceforth, all such archival citations refer to the Furlong Papers.
1 Barthes, *Mourning Diary*, 53.
2 Jansen, "Massive Iceberg Looms off Greenland Coast."
3 Tsing, "On Nonscalability," 505.
4 For an important discussion about modernity's logics, see Arturo Escobar's "In the Background of Our Culture," in *Designs for the Pluriverse*.
5 van Dooren, *Flight Ways*, 12.
6 For the past several years, I have been thinking about wonder with Andrea Ballestero. She uses wonder as a key concept to understand how water activists, scientists, and others position water as a human right in Costa Rica and Brazil. Ballestero justifies wonder as an analytic by saying, "In philosophical terms, wonder takes over when knowledge and understanding cannot master what they should" (*A Future History of Water*, x). For a discussion of wonder within philosophy, see Rubenstein, *Strange Wonder*. Tulasi Srinivas's *The Cow in the Elevator* is a very helpful example of allowing ethnographic research to shape wonder as an analytic.
7 Greenblatt, *Marvelous Possessions*.
8 Darwin, *Journal of Researches*, 503.

9 For a discussion of Darwin's wonder, see Philip Armstrong, "The Wonderment of This Taxonomy," 161.
10 Marcos Mendoza writes, "Patagonian tourists experience the sublime as a sense of wonderment, intense connection, and even rapture before the majesty of the Andean wilderness, a sentiment that they take back home with them, where it works to recruit the next wave of travelers" (*The Patagonian Sublime*, 5).
11 *Fueguinos: Fotografías siglos XIX y XX*, edited by Álvarado P. et al., is a wonderful collection of essays about the power and circulation of Fuegian images.
12 The "lost tribes" trope is similar to and as damaging as the "first contact" narratives Lucas Bessire describes in *Behold the Black Caiman*, a comparison I found helpful in writing this book.
13 Kyle Whyte makes this point in "Indigenous Science (Fiction) for the Anthropocene" more broadly, arguing that the literature on climate change and the Anthropocene often positions Indigenous peoples in historicized temporal categories. This framing, he argues, enables non-Indigenous allies to position themselves as saviors, without the burden of acknowledging their ancestors' roles in the making of the present.
14 Srinivas was surprised to discover wonder in the performative excesses on display in the temples of Bangalore, where she was doing fieldwork. Wonder, she found, is generated in sites that lie between the past (one defined by neoliberalism's crushing and persistent losses) and hope for a different future. In her account of ritual performances, wonder is both a practice of "amazement" as well as "a tiny space of resistance that stands within the brokenness and precarity of everyday life in the city" (*The Cow in the Elevator*, 4).
15 Tsing's *The Mushroom at the End of the World* has taught me to pay attention to what survives even in the midst of capitalist and colonial destruction.
16 Donna Haraway offers the hopeful slogan "We are all lichens" as a model for living well with other creatures among the rocks (*Staying with the Trouble*, 56).
17 Guanacos are one of the largest mammals in South America, closely related to llamas.
18 Solnit, *Hope in the Dark*, 5.
19 Pratt defines "contact zones" as "social spaces where disparate cultures meet, clash, and grapple with each other, often in highly asymmetrical relations of domination and subordination—like colonialism, slavery, or their aftermaths as they are lived across the globe today" (*Imperial Eyes*, 4).
20 In anthropology and history, there is a wonderful body of scholarship that critically interrogates the structure and logics of colonial archives, particularly Ann Laura Stoler's work on Dutch colonial archives. In *Along the Archival Grain*, Stoler insists that we see colonial archives as sites where enlightenment and exploitation are "deeply entangled projects." Her work has helped me approach the Furlong Papers as a site for understanding the representational logics of settler colonialism.

21 Maura Finkelstein has a beautifully written ethnography, *The Archive of Loss*. In it, she similarly extends the term *archive* to encompass nontraditional sites, including deindustrialized mills and mill worker bodies in Mumbai, that chronicle processes of industrial decline.

22 Vilém Flusser and Louis Bec's book *Vampyroteuthis infernalis* has been a longtime model and inspiration for my approach to multispecies speculations. The book is a serious yet incredibly fun and clever philosophical treatise on human subjectivity and existence told from the perspective of a vampire squid. Flusser's approach to philosophy was influenced by phenomenology, and his attention to how existence is shaped by embodied epistemologies has influenced my own interest in understanding how nonhumans sense and know their worlds, as well as in experimental approaches to evoking nonhuman subjectivities in writing.

23 Stengers, "Diderot's Egg," 11.

24 Stengers, "Including Nonhumans in Political Theory."

25 Stengers, *Cosmopolitics I*, 13.

26 Stengers, "Wondering about Materialism," 378. I am indebted to Gregory Seigworth and Melissa Gregg's thoughtful essay "An Inventory of Shimmers," which helped me think about affect in relation to Stengers's work. As they say of Stengers's writing, "Here affect is the hinge where mutable matter and wonder (ofttimes densely intermingled with world-weary dread too) perpetually tumble into each other" (8).

The Explorer's Refrain

Figure F2.1 is from MSS-197, Box VIII, Folder 3. Figure F2.2 is from MSS-197, Box XII, Folder 40. Figure F2.3 is from MSS-19, Box II, Folder 58.

1 Derrida describes "archive fever" as "burn[ing] with a passion. It is never to rest, interminably, from searching for the archive right where it slips away.... It is to have a compulsive, repetitive, and nostalgic desire for the archive, an irrepressible desire to return to the origin, a homesickness, a nostalgia for the return to the most archaic place of absolute commencement" (*Archive Fever*, 91).

2 The Furlong Papers was gifted to Dartmouth College by William E. Clark, and his gift included support for Furlong's efforts.

3 Royle, "Exploration," 676.

4 The letter can be found in MSS-197, Box I, Folder 10; emphasis added.

5 Crystal Fraser and Zoe Todd discuss the challenges of archives "produced by non-indigenous people: namely white men who dominated exploration, political and other 'great men' tropes," as sources for Indigenous history ("Decolonial Sensibilities," 35). As I hope is clear in this book, I am treating the archive as a source for understanding colonialism in Tierra del Fuego, its representational logics, and inscription practices, though the archive also provides insights into the white men who dominated exploration.

6 MSS-197, Box XII, Folder 40.
7 Taussig, *Fieldwork Notebooks*, 5.
8 Quotation found in Notebook 7, MSS-197, Box II, Folder 59.

Chapter One. The Earth as Archive

Figure 1.1 is from MSS-197, Box XIV, Folder 47. Figure 1.2 is from MSS-197, Box XXXVII and Box XXXVIII. Figure 1.3 is from MSS-197, Box X, Folder 38. Figure 1.4 is from MSS-197, Box XXXVIII, Folder 7. Figure 1.6 is a modified map from MSS-197, Box XXIV, Folder 3. Figure 1.9 is from MSS-197, Box X, Folder 36. Figure 1.10 (*left image*) is from MSS-197, Box IX, Folder 27. Figure 1.11 is from MSS-197, Box IX, Folder 31.

1 For a short description of the dermatoglyphs, see Mavalwala, "A Note on the Dermatoglyphics." Furlong describes obtaining the prints in "Brief Notes on the Furlong Collections." For a discussion of their history within anthropological research, see Jantz, "Anthropological Dermatoglyphic Research."
2 This quote can be found in the caption of a photograph found in MSS-197, Box X, Folder 38.
3 Furlong offers different spellings for the names of his Yagán and Selk'nam guides and other Indigenous people throughout the collection. I have chosen to use the variants published in a series of articles Furlong wrote for *Harper's Magazine*, mainly because the articles were written shortly after his expedition (when pronunciations were most likely still fresh in his mind). That said, his spelling variations often differ from other accounts from the era.
4 Furlong describes using the frying pan in a photo caption found in MSS-197, Box X, Folder 23.
5 George Stocking, the historian of anthropology, has described social evolutionism as "both the reflection of and the justification for the invasion, appropriation, and subjugation" of lands in colonial contexts ("Colonial Situations," 4). Furlong's scientific practices were clearly informed by social evolutionism and its popular variants, such as eugenics. In the mid-1960s, he shared his dermatoglyphs with Mavalwala, a biological anthropologist and expert in dermatoglyphics. For Mavalwala, and for Furlong too, it is the mere existence of the prints that establishes their value, because as Mavalwala put it, "the data on these two extinct groups are quite meagre" ("A Note on the Dermatoglyphics," 5–6). In these intellectual communities, the inky afterlife of Fuegian women, men, and children became rare data in the science of human biological variation.
6 Galton, *Finger Prints*, 23, 150.
7 Galton, *Finger Prints*, 2.
8 Galton, *Finger Prints*, 2.
9 Galton, *Finger Prints*, 2, 22, 98.

10 In "Clues," a wonderful essay, Carlo Ginzburg argues that historical research is a "conjectural paradigm" based on the interpretation of fragments. In this essay, Ginzburg also discusses Galton's interest in fingerprints.
11 Document titled "Furlong Sub-Antarctic Collection of Footprints and Handprints of Southernmost Autochthonous Inhabitants of the World," found in MSS-197, Box XXXVII, Folder 1.
12 I am grateful to my colleague Jeremy DeSilva for helping me with the trace fossil literature. For discussion of trace fossils, see Prothero, *Bringing Fossils to Life*, 419. Prothero notes that trace fossils are also called "ichnofossils," for the Greek *ichnos* translates as "trace."
13 Leakey, "Footprints in the Ashes of Time," 453.
14 Leakey, "Footprints in the Ashes of Time," 454.
15 For a discussion of how Derrida twists the term *trace* against its ordinary French connotations (as footprints or tracks), see Miller "Trace." Miller writes, "The trace is the non-presence of the present, which means the trace undoes the metaphysical or logocentric concept of time as made up of a present which is present here and now, a past which was once present and future which will one day be present" (49).
16 Judith Butler, introduction, xi.
17 Information found in Notebook 4, MSS-197, Box II, Folder 58.
18 Information found in Notebook 6, MSS-197, Box II, Folder 59.
19 Everything I know about affect comes from reading Kathleen Stewart's *Ordinary Affects* (as well as much that I value in ethnographic writing). I found Susan Lepselter's use of the term *resonance* extremely helpful as I was thinking through the dermatoglyphs. Lepselter uses resonance as a theory of connection, based on resemblance and repetition, that is felt (*The Resonance of Unseen Things*, 4).
20 For a thorough historical account of this story, see Hazlewood, *Savage*. For information about Darwin's time in the archipelago, see Rozzi and Heidinger, *The Route of Darwin*.
21 For a detailed critique of Darwin's representations of Yagán people, see Chapman, *European Encounters with the Yamana People*, chapter 4.
22 Chapman, *European Encounters with the Yamana People*, 612.
23 Darwin, *The Autobiography*, 76.
24 Darwin, *The Autobiography*, 72.
25 Darwin, *Journal of Researches*, 233.
26 For a discussion of Darwin's contributions to ornithology, see Steinheimer, "Charles Darwin's Bird Collection."
27 In addition to these geologic features, there are numerous species named after the naturalist, including Darwin's rhea (*Rhea pennata*), also called the lesser rhea, an ostrich-type bird that roams that Patagonian steppe, and an edible fungus, *Cyttaria darwinii*, commonly called Indian bread.
28 Chapman, *European Encounters with the Yamana People*, 5.
29 Chapman, *European Encounters with the Yamana People*, i.

30 Chapman, *European Encounters with the Yamana People*, 596.
31 I am indebted to Tania Murray Li for the term *inscription*, which she used in a paper presented at the American Anthropological Association meetings in 2014. The paper, "Territory, Belonging and the Work of Inscription on an Indigenous Land Frontier," examines the mapping of customary communities in the Lauje highlands of Central Sulawesi. Throughout the world, colonialism is enacted through predictable inscription practices, such as the transformation of land and life into property and resources, simultaneous to the destruction and displacement of Indigenous lives and worlds, as occurred in the Fuegian Archipelago and throughout North America. Inscription practices associated with settler colonialism also include ways of inscribing identity, with practices such as "playing Indian," as Philip Deloria makes clear; US racial categories imposed through blood quantum and "Native American" DNA logics, as Circe Sturm examined in *Blood Politics* and Kim TallBear shows in *Native American DNA*; as well as the transformation of sovereignty claims into "civil rights" (see Tuck and Yang, "Decolonization Is Not a Metaphor"). Introduced animal and plant life has been bound up in the apparatus of settler colonialism, a process Alfred Crosby calls *ecological imperialism*, yet this is certainly an inscription practice.
32 Taussig, *Mimesis and Alterity*, 87.
33 In this section of the book, I refer to Orundelico as "Jemmy Button" as a way of signaling a distinction between a real person (Orundelico) and a colonial fantasy (Jemmy Button). For a wonderful ethnography exploring the coloniality of "massacre stories," see Cameron, *Far Off Metal River*.
34 "Bahía Wulaia," Wikipedia, accessed December 15, 2019, https://en.wikipedia.org/wiki/Bah%C3%ADa_Wulaia.
35 Bridges, *Uttermost Part of the Earth*, 43.
36 For example, Bridges said, "It was subsequently established beyond all reasonable doubt that Jimmy Button had been the chief instigator of the massacre" (*Uttermost Part of the Earth*, 46).
37 Quote can be found in Notebook 10, MSS-197, Box II, Folder 59.
38 Furlong says that Fortunato Beban, who captained Furlong's hired sloop, pointed out the gravesite to him. When he arrived, the grave was marked by a weathered stump. Furlong took a blurry photograph of the grave marker, which can be found in MSS-197, Box IX, Folder 29.
39 Bridges, *Uttermost Part of the Earth*, 84.
40 Furlong, "Some Effects of Environment on the Fuegian Tribes," 180.
41 I am not sure how, but Furlong seems to have met Vrsalovic while he was in Ushuaia a few weeks before traveling to Wulaia. See Notebook 2, MSS-197, Box II, Folder 58.
42 Photograph caption, MSS-197, Box III, Folder 26.
43 Marisol de la Cadena offers the concept of "co-laboring" to describe thinking and learning together across difference, while not collapsing difference (epistemological, ontological, historical) into anthropological explanation,

or, as she says, not "pretending to replace my common sense, but also preventing it from prevailing" (*Earth Beings*, 16). I have found her discussion an incredibly helpful source for thinking critically about knowledge hierarchies and ethnographic writing.

Arturo Escobar

1 For a discussion of the political ecology of mud, see Cortesi, "The Muddy Semiotics of Mud."
2 Escobar, *Designs for the Pluriverse*.

The Archival Earth

Figure F4.1 is from MSS-197, Box VIII, Folders 35 and 37.

1 In "Patchy Anthropocene," Tsing and others move beyond critique of the Anthropocene concept to ask (and show) what anthropology can offer understandings of Anthropocene phenomena, as well as ask how Anthropocene debates challenge and transform anthropology. In particular, their intervention focuses attention on multispecies landscape histories and structures.
2 While debates continue, earth system scientists seem to be coming to a consensus that the Anthropocene began at the midpoint of the twentieth century. See Steffen et al., "The Trajectory of the Anthropocene"; Waters et al., "The Anthropocene Is Functionally and Stratigraphically Distinct from the Holocene"; Zalasiewicz et al., "The Geological Cycle of Plastics." In an earlier piece, "The Anthropocene," Steffen, Crutzen, and McNeill offer a model of a staged Anthropocene, with the industrial era (ca. 1800–1945) as the first stage and the postwar "Great Acceleration" as the second stage. Ellis discusses the Anthropocene Working Group's process of consensus in *Anthropocene*, 74. Smith and Zeder offer an alternative perspective on the Anthropocene's beginning, suggesting the Pleistocene-Holocene boundary, in "The Onset of the Anthropocene." Of course, human activities have been remaking the earth for thousands of years. The domestication of plant and animal life, the development of agriculture in multiple parts of the world, fire regimes, and the hunting of megafauna—these have all produced landscape-scale impacts on the earth and the earth's ecosystems. See Swanson, Lien, and Ween, *Domestication Gone Wild* for a wonderful reexamination of domestication. Yet it is clear that capitalism's postwar intensification and the Atomic Age have left unprecedented inscriptions on the earth and our atmosphere.
3 Hadfield and Haraway, "The Tree Snail Manifesto."
4 Ellis, *Anthropocene*, 35.
5 Formal recognition of the Anthropocene as a unit of stratigraphic time requires finding traces of human impacts in the earth's sediments and ice that

demonstrate that the present is distinct, as Ellis clearly states: "The methods of stratigraphy are clear. Transformative changes in the Earth system are not enough. To appear in the Geologic Time Scale, an event must leave the right kind of stratigraphic evidence" (*Anthropocene*, 43). Waters and colleagues provide a comprehensive inventory of the Anthropocene's stratigraphic evidence, what they call "stratigraphic signatures" ("The Anthropocene Is Functionally and Stratigraphically Distinct from the Holocene," 137). Their analysis leaves little doubt that the earth itself has changed. What they found: radioactive residues from nuclear testing have created a global signal of the Cold War's "bomb spike"; petrochemical traces in ice and soil act as depositions, literally, of an earth distinct from the Holocene; novel materials, such as aluminum, concrete, and plastics, now characterize the earth's rocks, soil, and sea; accumulations of nitrogen and phosphorus inventory the past century's increase in fertilizer use; ice cores and tree rings now register the shifting concentrations of atmospheric CO_2, the result of burning fossil hydrocarbons.

6   Knoblauch, "The Environmental Toll of Plastics."
7   As Zalasiewicz et al. write, "Most of the global plastics that have been produced are still present in the environment" ("The Geological Cycle of Plastics," 5). David Barnes, a researcher for the British Antarctic Survey, and colleagues have described plastic's impacts on the surface of earth in "Accumulation and Fragmentation of Plastic Debris in Global Environments."
8   Lewis and Maslin, "Defining the Anthropocene," 175.
9   Davis and Todd, "On the Importance of a Date," 769. In "The Inhuman Anthropocene" Luciano argues that these ice cores reconfigure "what story can and should be told about human impact on the planet."
10 Stratigraphic time has the characteristics of what Michael Serres calls a classical theory of time. His critique of classical theories of time reminds me of the stratigraphic earth's linearity, saying of classical time, "Instead of inhabiting the heart or the middle of the world, we are sojourning at the summit, the height, the best of truth" (*Conversations on Science, Culture, and Time*, 45).
11 Here I am alluding to Walter Benjamin's famous evocation of the "angel of history," who is caught in a storm, its wings forced open, its back turned to the future, as it stares backward at a growing pile of wreckage. Benjamin says the storm is "what we call progress" ("Theses on the Philosophy of History," 257).
12 Stratigraphic time is a way of constituting commonality, or a universal ontology of the world and history, in de la Cadena's formulation in "Uncommons."
13 Contributors to *Arts of Living on a Damaged Planet*, edited by Tsing et al., offer thought-provoking essays that examine, in part, the multiple temporalities that are wrapped up in multispecies encounters.
14 There is more to the archival earth's stratigraphic logic worth noticing, as

I have learned from Elizabeth Povinelli, Kathryn Yusoff, and Kim TallBear. In *Geontologies* Povinelli extends and complicates Foucault's biopolitics to account for contemporary settler modes of distinguishing and governing life and nonlife, as well as for the ways Indigenous Australian ontologies reconfigure this binary. Building from Povinelli, the organizing logic of the archival earth, at least in its stratigraphic rendering, is geontological. Povinelli asserts that geology, the intellectual foundation for the stratigraphic earth, finds its intellectual home in earthy versions of extractive capitalism. She describes the exploitation of the coalfields in Europe that revealed large stratified fossil beds that helped spur the modern geologic chronology. She goes on to say, "The concept of the Anthropocene is as much a product of the coalfields as an analysis of their formation insofar as the fossils within the coalfields helped produce and secure the modern discipline of geology and by contrast biology" (9). The stratigraphic earth tells a story of geos (earth) archiving the losses of bios (animals, plants, and humans), leaving no room for layers of rock (nonlife) to be kin. Yusoff, in her brilliant *A Billion Black Anthropocenes or None*, has taught me how the stratigraphic version of the archival earth is a legacy of white geography—a legacy blind to the racial and colonial violence that constitutes the present. TallBear, in "Beyond the Life/Not-Life Binary," a discussion of the cryopreservation of genetic material, offers a careful critique of the living and nonliving binary that dominates non-Indigenous ontologies and ethics, as well as an important intervention into various strands of relational philosophy that continues to define "life" using organismal categories.

15 See Wolfe, "Settler Colonialism and the Elimination of the Native." In this essay, Wolfe defines settler colonialism as a form of colonialism whose central logic is the acquisition of territory through the displacement and removal of Indigenous peoples.

16 Achille Mbembe richly describes the temporalities of postcolonialism as "entangled." The time of entanglement, he says, is an "interlocking of presents, pasts, and futures that retain their depths of other presents, pasts, and futures, each age bearing, altering, and maintaining the previous ones" (*On the Postcolony*, 16).

Chapter Two. Alternative Archives of the Present

Figure 2.1 is from MSS-197, Box XIV, Folder 18.

1 There are very few specimens of Fuegian dogs, though descriptions abound in explorer and ethnographic accounts. See Snow, "A Few Remarks on the Wild Tribes of Tierra del Fuego," and Bridges, *Uttermost Part of the Earth*, 101. Romina Petrigh and Martín Fugassa conducted DNA analysis of one of the few specimens of Fuegian dogs and confirmed that they descend from culpeo fox rather than the domestic dog: "Molecular Identification of a Fuegian Dog."

2 Derrida, *Archive Fever*, 4.
3 For a rich and nuanced account of Dartmouth's history, see Colin Calloway, *The Indian History of an American Institution*.
4 Donna Haraway's "Teddy Bear Patriarchy" has forever changed the way I experience natural history museums.
5 Allentoft et al., "Extinct New Zealand Megafauna," 4922.
6 Jarvis, "The Obsessive Search for the Tasmanian Tiger."
7 Other attempts have been more successful. My father, an ornithologist, was part of the research team that brought the last wild California condor into captivity in 1987 to live at the San Diego Zoo. AC-9, as the condor was called, was released fifteen years later, after a successful captive breeding program slowed the species' rapid progress toward extinction.
8 Heatherington, "Seeds."
9 Esther Breithoff and Rodney Harrison have called these genetic archiving efforts "speculative reinvestment" ("From Ark to Bank," 38).
10 Chile is second only to Norway in farmed salmon production. The similarity of the countries' coastal environments led the Pinochet administration to pursue salmon farming as an economic development strategy during the early 1980s. While these salmon farms are physically located in Chile, the Chilean industry reflects the complexities (and concealments) of multinational corporate structures. Chile's neoliberal regulatory system has encouraged this multinational investment and enabled the overuse of antibiotics, disease outbreaks, and catastrophic environmental impacts, particularly toxic algal blooms. For a thorough history and analysis of farmed salmon in Chile, see Soluri, "Something Fishy." Information about the market structure of Chilean salmon farming can be found in Gonzalez Poblete et al., "The Impact of Trade and Markets on Chilean Atlantic Salmon Farming." For analysis of the environmental impacts of Chilean salmon farming, see Quiñones et al., "Environmental Issues in Chilean Salmon Farming." For example, the Norwegian Marine Harvest corporation, the world's largest producer of farmed salmon, has a subsidiary in Chile. Marine Harvest was recently sanctioned after several hundred thousand of its Atlantic salmon escaped into the wild off Chile's southern coastal town of Calbuco (Sherwood, "Chile Regulator Charges Marine Harvest with Environmental Breaches").
11 Prior to the protests, many Chileans were unaware that Fuegian Indigenous people still lived in the archipelago. For the community itself, these protests were one of the most unifying and dramatic political events in the community's recent history. A copy of the letter can be found at "The Yagan's Letter to the King of Norway: 'Don't Install This Destructive Industry in Our Territory,'" *Patagon Journal*.
12 "The Yagan's Letter to the King of Norway: 'Don't Install This Destructive Industry in Our Territory,'" *Patagon Journal*.
13 For a comprehensive discussion about the historical processes that have

come to define Indigenous-state relations in Chile, see Di Giminiani, *Sentient Lands*.

Lichens on the Beach

1 Brandt et al., "Viability of the Lichen *Xanthoria elegans*."
2 Sancho, "Lichens and Their Habitats," 155.
3 Sancho, "Lichens and Their Habitats," 180.
4 Yong, "The Overlooked Organisms."
5 Pringle, "Establishing New Worlds," G157.
6 Plitt, "A Short History of Lichenology," 78.
7 Plitt, "A Short History of Lichenology," 81.
8 Crustose lichens grow more slowly than other forms, averaging less than 0.5 mm per year, according to Richard Armstrong, "Lichens, Lichenometry and Global Warming," 33.
9 Benedict, "A Review of Lichenometric Dating," 143.
10 Pringle "Establishing New Worlds"; see also Nuwer, "Lichens Do Not Age."
11 Galloway, "Phytogeography of Southern Hemisphere Lichens," 199.

Chapter Three. An Empire of Skin

Parts of this chapter appeared in "The Beaver Diaspora: A Thought Experiment," *Environmental Humanities* 10, no. 1 (2018): 63–85; and "Saturate," in *Veer Ecology: A Companion for Environmental Thinking*, edited by Jeffrey Jerome Cohen and Lowell Duckert (Minneapolis: University of Minnesota Press, 2017), 297–311.

Figure 3.3 is from MSS-197, Box XXIV, Folder 3. Figure 3.5 is from MSS-197, Box X, Folder 47. Figure 3.6 is from MSS-197, Box X, Folder 45.

1 This project was curated by Camila Marambio, as part of the *Ensayos* research collective, which I discuss later in this book.
2 This quote can be found in Journal 4, MSS-197, Box II, Folder 58.
3 Anderson et al., "Do Introduced North American Beavers *Castor canadensis* Engineer Differently in Southern South America?"
4 For decades, the role of invasive species has been central to discussions of environmental loss (Vitousek et al., "Biological Invasions as Global Environmental Change," 468). Research in the biosciences shows a strong correlation between animal extinctions and invasive species, with projected changes in climate accelerating rates of species extinctions (Clavero and García-Berthous, "Invasive Species Are a Leading Cause of Animal Extinctions," 110; Thomas et al., "Extinction Risk from Climate Change"). "Biotic exchange" is now considered one of the top five causes of biodiversity loss in the world, particularly in freshwater ecosystems (Sala et al., "Global Biodiversity Scenarios for the Year 2100"). Yet even within conservation communities, the invasive species paradigm is being challenged on conceptual,

political, and ethical grounds. For a discussion of these debates, see Davis et al., "Don't Judge Species on Their Origins"; and Simberloff et al., "Nonnatives." See also Chew and Hamilton, "The Rise and Fall of Biotic Nativeness"; Chew, "Ecologists, Environmentalists, Experts"; and Reo and Ogden, "Anishnaabe Aki."

5 Understanding why certain species are considered objects (and therefore "killable") rather than subjects (and less killable) has been central to posthumanist philosophy and associated scholarship. See Erica Fudge's *Animal*, Donna Haraway's *When Species Meet*, and Patricia Lopez and Kathryn Gillespie's *Economies of Death*.

6 In "Being Prey," Val Plumwood describes how her attack by a crocodile transformed her understanding of what constitutes the human in relation to other prey animals.

7 For discussions of origin, mobility, return, and home, see Avtar Brah's *Cartographies of Diaspora*, James Clifford's "Diasporas," and Kim Butler's "Defining Diaspora, Refining a Discourse."

8 Marienne Lien and John Law in "Emergent Aliens" have examined how salmon aquaculture in Norway redefine categories of wild and domesticated. Based on ethnographic work in Mexican genetic labs, John Hartigan argues in "Mexican Genomics and the Roots of Racial Thinking" that racial thinking extends beyond humans to shape ideas about the nature of species. In "Invasive Narratives and the Inverse of Slow Violence" Susanna Lidström and colleagues argue that "invasive narratives" efface socioecological complexity in ways that may ultimately exacerbate environmental problems, while in "The Potential Conservation Value of Non-native Species," M. A. Schlaepfer, D. F. Sax, and J. D. Olden have demonstrated the conservation benefits of nonnative species.

9 Hall, "Culture Identity and Diaspora," 236.

10 Hintzen and Rahier, "Introduction: Theorizing the African Diaspora."

11 For an overview of diaspora scholarship, see Rogers Brubaker's "The Diaspora' Diaspora." For work on the politics of diaspora subjectivity, see Paul Gilroy's *"There Ain't No Black in the Union Jack"* and "Cultural Studies and Ethnic Absolutism," as well as Jacqueline Nassy Brown's *Dropping Anchor, Setting Sail*.

12 See Rahier, "Blackness, the Racial/Spatial Order, Migrations, and Miss Ecuador 1995–96"; and Venn, "Identity, Diasporas, and Subjective Change."

13 Pietrek and Fasola, "Origin and History of the Beaver Introduction in South America."

14 Examples include the introduction of Arctic foxes on the Aleutian Islands; mink, muskrat, and rabbits in Europe; and nutria in the United States.

15 Important discussions about the racial and xenophobic valences of the invasive species rhetoric can be found in Banu Subramaniam's "Aliens Have Landed!," Brendon Larson's "The War of the Roses," Jean Comaroff and John Comaroff's "Naturing the Nation," Hugh Raffles's "Mother Nature's

Melting Pot," and Paul Robbins and Sarah Moore's "Ecological Anxiety Disorder."

16 MSS-197, Box II, Folder 57; emphasis added.
17 For a wonderful oral history of the Caleta María sawmill, see Samuel García O.'s "Vestigios patrimoniales del aserradero Caleta María."
18 Since the Pinochet dictatorship, economic growth in Chile has been reliant on the export of natural resources, as we discuss in Mendoza et al., "The Patagonian Imaginary," 105. The transition to a deregulated economy and neoliberal economic system particularly impacted Chile's forests, though plantation forestry and related industries have been central to Chile's environmental history since the 1930s and key to the making of the modern Chilean state (Klubock, "The Politics of Forests and Forestry"). Klubock's account of southern Chile's environmental history situates regional deforestation as integral to larger cycles of settlement, colonization, and related transitions to agriculture.
19 Ginn, *Investing in Nature*.
20 Houck, *Taking Back Eden*.
21 Klepeis and Laris, "Contesting Sustainable Development in Tierra del Fuego."
22 Houck, *Taking Back Eden*.
23 An account of this history can be found at Whidbey Environmental Action Network, "WEAN's History with Trillium Corp."
24 Terre Satterfield in *Anatomy of a Conflict* and Sarah Pike in *For the Wild* offer important ethnographic accounts of the "forest wars" of the Pacific Northwest.
25 For an overview of Chilean environmentalism, see Carruthers, "Environmental Politics in Chile." As Carruthers explains, Chilean environmental organizations have tended to focus on issues of native forest decline. The political coalition that formed immediately following the return to democracy had some links to environmental organizations, giving them some influence, but this quickly waned as Chilean politics transformed into a highly centralized system of elite consensus in which political decisions were made within a relatively closed circle of political, business, and other elites, a circle to which environmental groups have struggled to gain entry. See also Tecklin, Bauer, and Prieto, "Making Environmental Law for the Market"; and Sepúlveda and Villaroel, "Swans, Conflicts, and Resonance." Government policy and the system of environmental impact assessment has consistently favored large infrastructure and extractive industry projects despite environmental concerns, as both papers describe. For example, President Eduardo Frei (1994–2000) stated, "No project will be stopped for environmental considerations" (quoted in Rojas et al., "Conflictos ambientales en Chile") and that the purpose of the environmental impact assessment system was to approve, not prevent, major development projects.

26 Houck, *Taking Back Eden*; Klepeis and Laris, "Contesting Sustainable Development in Tierra del Fuego."
27 Whidbey Environmental Action Network, "WEAN's History with Trillium Corp."
28 Ginn says that Henry Paulson, Goldman's CEO at the time, asked the Nature Conservancy (TNC) to evaluate the value of the Trillium lands, most likely due to TNC's prior experience with bankrupt forestry projects in Chile and because Paulson served on TNC's board. TNC staff, both legal and environmental, brought their expertise to bear upon the task of evaluating the conservation value of Trillium's property in Chile. Though TNC played a key role in Goldman's calculus, the two organizations decided early on, according to Ginn, that because Paulson served on both boards, this conflict of interest would prevent TNC from acquiring the Trillium lands (*Investing in Nature*, 61). The decision was also influenced by a considerable public relations crisis for TNC that emerged during this period, following a series of articles in the *Washington Post* that were highly critical of TNC's leadership, practices, and strategy.
29 The Wildlife Conservation Society is one of the world's most recognized conservation organizations. Founded in 1895, it manages conservation programs on four continents, as well as a mammoth urban park system in New York City that includes the Bronx Zoo, the Central Park Zoo, and the New York Aquarium.
30 In *Ecological Imperialism*, Crosby uses the term *neo-Europes* to describe the social and ecological transformation of New Zealand, Australia, most of North America, and the pampas of South America associated with European settlement.
31 Wolfe, "Settler Colonialism and the Elimination of the Native."
32 Excerpt from photo caption, MSS-197, Box XII, Folder 45.
33 Bridges, *Uttermost Part of the Earth*, 147. Today Harberton remains in the Bridges family and looks much the same, though there is a restaurant and museum on site for tourists. In 2013, I interviewed Natalie Goodall, then the matriarch of the family, at Harberton. Goodall was from the United States, drawn to Tierra del Fuego after reading Bridges's *Uttermost Part of the Earth*. Unlike others similarly captivated, Goodall married the author's great-nephew. She remained at Harberton for the rest of her life, raising her daughters and becoming a keen and celebrated naturalist, particularly of marine life.
34 Information contained in the photograph caption, MSS-197, Box IX, Folder 22, and also found in a small diary, MSS-197, Box II, Folder 56.
35 Furlong describes the Yagán labor at Remolino, saying there were about twenty Yagán shepherds employed by the Lawrences, while women were employed carding wool; see diary in MSS-197, Box II, Folder 56.
36 Bridges, *Uttermost Part of the Earth*, 100.

37 Jaksic and Yañez, "Rabbit and Fox Introductions in Tierra del Fuego"; Davis and DeMello, *Stories Rabbits Tell*.
38 Silva and Saavedra, "Knowing for Controlling."
39 Klepeis and Laris, "Hobby Ranching and Chile's Land-Reform Legacy," 381.
40 Butland, *The Human Geography of Southern Chile*; Martinic B., "The Meeting of Two Cultures."
41 Klepeis and Laris, "Hobby Ranching and Chile's Land-Reform Legacy."
42 Subramaniam, "The Aliens Have Landed!," 35.
43 In "Post-establishment Changes in Habitat Selection by an Invasive Species," Alejandro Pietrek and Mariano González-Roglich provide an insightful analysis of the beaver establishment on the pampas of Tierra del Fuego. They conducted their research at Estancia Sara, on the Argentine side of the island.
44 Pietrek and González-Roglich, "Post-establishment Changes in Habitat Selection by an Invasive Species," 3226.
45 Crosby, *Ecological Imperialism*.
46 Pietrek and Fasola, "Origin and History of the Beaver Introduction in South America."
47 Bridges, *Uttermost Part of the Earth*, 85.
48 Bridges, *Uttermost Part of the Earth*, 189.
49 Tsing, *The Mushroom at the End of the World*, 23.
50 C. S. Holling and Gary Meffe referred to this as "command and control" forms of natural resource management ("Command and Control and the Pathology of Natural Resource Management").
51 Haraway says, "Staying with the trouble requires learning to be truly present, not as a vanishing pivot between awful or Edenic pasts and apocalyptic or salvific futures, but as mortal critters entwined in myriad unfinished configurations of places, times, matters, meanings" (*Staying with the Trouble*, 1).
52 See examples of this body of work at the Ensayos website, http://ensayos tierradelfuego.net. I discuss some of this performance work in chapter 5 of this book.

The Anthropologist

Figure F6.1 is from MSS-197, Box VIII, Folder 11. Figure F6.2 is from MSS-197, Box XII, Folder 49. Figure F6.3 is from MSS-197, Box XIV, Folder 15.
1 Much of the material in the Furlong Papers at Dartmouth, including his journals and photographs, concerns Selk'nam, Yagán, Haush, and Kawésqar communities in the Fuegian Archipelago, as well as the Tehuelche communities of southern Patagonia.
2 Furlong, "Brief Notes on the Furlong Collections," 463.
3 Furlong, "Exploration in Tierra del Fuego and the Fuegian Archipelago," 221.
4 This quote can be found in the entry for January 7, 1908, MSS-197, Box II, Folder 57.

5   For example, Furlong presented and published two ethnographic descriptions of Fuegian peoples as part of the nineteenth International Congress of Americanists, held in Washington, DC, in 1915. In 1916 he provided "Map of Tierra del Fuego Showing Some Ona, Yahan, and Haush Settlement Sites Definitely Located by the Furlong Exhibition of 1907–08 and 1910." This map was used by Samuel K. Lothrop on an expedition funded by the Museum of the American Indian; see MSS-197, Box VIII, Folder 7. Lothrop's participation caught the attention of scholars interested in the region, in particular John M. Cooper, a Catholic priest who became a prominent American anthropologist. Cooper's first substantial work was a comprehensive review of everything known about Fuegian peoples. "Analytical and Critical Bibliography" relied heavily on Furlong's expertise as "our foremost North American authority" on the topic, and the manuscript references Furlong 122 times. Without a doubt, Cooper's review enabled a career pivot for Furlong, leading to Furlong's incorporation into a small but international community of Fuegian scholars.

6   A nice biography of Gusinde can be found on the *Anthropos* website; see "Martin Gusinde SVD," accessed December 22, 2020, https://www.anthropos.eu/anthropos/heritage/gusinde.php.

7   Maturana Díaz, "Fotografía antropológica de Charles Wellington Furlong," 56.

8   The historian Marisol Palma Behnke recently transcribed and published Gusinde's journals from his Tierra del Fuego research trips: "Diario del primer viaje de Martín Gusinde a Tierra del Fuego (1918–1919)" and "Diario del segundo viaje de Martín Gusinde a Fuego Patagonia (1919–1920)."

9   The Gusinde correspondence can be found in MSS-197, Box I, Folder 31.

10 The letter can be found in MSS-197, Box I, Folder 31.

11 For example, in 1929 Gusinde published an extensive bibliography of Central and South American anthropology, "Zentral-Amerika und Südamerika." In the section titled "Feuerland" he lists sixteen of his own articles and none of Furlong's publications.

Chapter Four. Stolen Images

Figures 4.1 and 4.2 are from negatives from MSS-197, Box XXIV, Folder 3. Figure 4.3 is from MSS-197, Box IX, Folder 50. Figure 4.4 is from MSS-197, Box XIV, Folder 46. Figure 4.5 is from MSS-197, Box XIV, Folder 5. Figure 4.6 (*left*) is from MSS-197, Box VIII, Folder 17; and (*right*) is from MSS-197, Box VIII, Folder 16. Figure 4.7 is from MSS-197, Box XIV, Folders 40 and 48. Figure 4.8 (*left*) is from MSS-197, Box XIII, Folder 47; and (*right*) is from MSS-197, Box XII, Folder 48. Figure 4.9 is from MSS-197, Box XXIV, Folder 3.

1   Today the value of the Furlong Papers for understanding the culture and history of Yagán and Selk'nam people is up to these communities. Certainly the images and their annotations provide insight into territorial practices

and claims, as well as documentation of some of the transformations in life, livelihoods, and relations that were occurring during the frontier stage of colonial settlement. During meetings about the collection, community members mainly expressed interest in identifying the identities of relatives and confirming the accuracy of locations and sites represented in the images. This is a separate project, not mine to publish, but one that I am committed to continuing.

2 In the following decades, Furlong published and republished his iconic images everywhere. Sometimes they appeared in well-respected academic journals where he argued for increased protection for Fuegian peoples. His tone in more popular publications struck a different note, though the photographs are the same or similar. For example, in 1932 he wrote a series of six articles for the *Daily Express*, a British tabloid. He introduced the series by describing Tierra del Fuego as "inhabited by a race of wolflike men, the Onas and Yahgans, who rely for hunting on bows and arrows, and have no government, no writing, no education and no gods." The title of the first installment is "Unknown Race Which Defies Civilisation." These articles are archived in MSS-197, Box IX, Folder 16.

3 The Harper and Brothers corporation paid Furlong $500 per article, as well as $600 toward his trip expenses. Adjusted for inflation, this would be about $58,000 today, not an inconsequential amount. The *Harper's* contract secured the magazine's first publication rights for the images, though Furlong was able to republish the photographs in later publications. Correspondence and Furlong's contract can be found in MSS-197, Box I, Folder 33. In "Fotografía antropólogica de Charles Wellington Furlong," Felipe Maturana Díaz describes the aesthetics of the *Harper's* images and compares them to Furlong's photographs published elsewhere.

4 For a discussion of Conrad's relationship with *Harper's*, see Ruppel, "Pathos and Fun."

5 This form of ethnographic authority has been referred to as "salvage anthropology." Born in the contact zones of colonialism, salvage anthropology was predicated on the idea that Indigenous cultures were going extinct and that anthropology's highest purpose was to document these cultures. As Jacob Gruber states, the specter of the "vanishing savage" transformed anthropology into an "amalgam of moral and scientific concerns" ("Ethnographic Salvage and the Shaping of Anthropology," 1294). Settler savior fantasies aside, Furlong was in Tierra del Fuego at the height of the Fuegian genocide, and the losses he witnessed were profound. His journals contain population data, much of it compiled from missionary estimates, that suggest a reduction in the Fuegian Indigenous population by about 80 percent within the fifty years prior to his visit. Furlong's journals also offer an unbearable catalog of violent acts: gunshot wounds, lynching, rapes, and the desecration of Selk'nam and Yagán bodies by bounty hunters. See also Legoupil, "The Population and Depopulation of Tierra del Fuego." During a

discussion of a section of this book manuscript, Sylvia Yanagisako helped me think about the ways contemporary environmental anthropology's concerns about environmental change and species extinctions mirror some of the rhetorical and ethical positions common to salvage anthropology of the nineteenth century.

6 Rosaldo, "Imperialist Nostalgia," 108.
7 See descriptions in Furlong, "Amid the Islands of the Land of Fire," "The Southernmost People in the World," and "Into the Unknown Land of the Onas."
8 Furlong, "The Vanishing People of the Land of Fire," 228.
9 Maturana Díaz, "Fotographía antropológica de Charles Wellington Furlong," notes the similarities of compositions in Fuegian photography. There is wonderful scholarship on the Fuegian photography of this era, including Furlong's contributions; see also Barthe, "*Uun-Daranata*," and Palma Behnke, "To Save What Is Left." Mateo Martinic Beros, the foremost historian of the region, says these Fuegian images continue to be popular because they act as a testament to losses in the making ("El acervo patrimonial de Tierra del Fuego," 13).
10 Furlong, "The Vanishing People of the Land of Fire."
11 Barthe, "*Uun-Daranata*," 14.
12 Zand, "An Introduction to Dualphotography."
13 Furlong, "Exploration in Tierra del Fuego and the Fuegian Archipelago," 220.
14 Pocket diary, entry dated June 7, 1907, MSS-197, Box II, Folder 56.
15 Pocket diary, entry dated February 15, 1907, MSS-197, Box II, Folder 56.
16 Eve Tuck and Wayne Yang have taught me to understand these strategies of exceptionalism as classic "moves to innocence," a fantasy when "the Native (understanding that he is becoming extinct) hands over his land, his claim to the land, his very Indian-ness to the settler for safe-keeping" ("Decolonization Is Not a Metaphor," 14).
17 Pocket diary, entry dated January 12, 1908, MSS-197, Box II, Folder 56.
18 Furlong, "Into the Unknown Land of the Onas," 443.
19 See Agamben, "What Is an Apparatus?," 20.
20 Of course, managing and ignoring these contradictions are part of the colonial apparatus's vernacular (just like loss and wonder), techniques that Pratt calls "anti-conquest" strategies (*Imperial Eyes*, 7).
21 Pocket diary, entry dated January 14, 1908, MSS-197, Box II, Folder 56.
22 Over a decade later, Gusinde made his first trip to Tierra del Fuego, visiting many of the same sites that Furlong had. First, Gusinde visited the Salesian mission La Candelaría, on the north side of the Rio Grande. At the mission, which Furlong also visited, Gusinde expressed disappointment at the Selk'nam residents' lack of cultural knowledge. He then traveled south to Najmishk, and like Furlong, he treated the site as an ethnographic museum. Palma Behnke, "To Save What Is Left," has said that Gusinde de-

scribed, at great length, the poverty he witnessed at Najmishk, even though this poverty is invisible in his photographs.

23   Furlong, "The Vanishing People of the Land of Fire," 220.
24   This information comes from Notebook 2, MSS-197, Box II, Folder 58. In "Recordando a un imperio pastoral" Martinic provides an excellent discussion of the *Sociedad Explotadora de Tierra del Fuego*'s history, operations, and legacies. He notes that at its height of operation, the company controlled over three million hectares of land.
25   Responding to Furlong's request, Mauricio Braun shipped the film across the Strait of Magellan to the small port of Porvenir on Tierra del Fuego. There, a gaucho on horseback carried the film across the island to Estancia Sara, a trip of several days.
26   Pocket diary, entry dated February 14, 1908, MSS-197, Box II, Folder 56.
27   Information about Andrew MacLellan can be found on this genealogy message board at Ancestry, accessed December 14, 2019, https://www.ancestry.co.uk/boards/surnames.maclennan/71/mb.ashx. Chatwin describes MacLellan as "a strong man, with a flat face reddened by whisky and the tropics, pale red hair and eyes, that flashed both blue and green" (*In Patagonia*, 117). Bridges (*Uttermost Part of the Earth*, 251) also discusses MacLellan, though he gives him the pseudonym "Mr. McInch."
28   Pocket diary, MSS-197, Box II, Folder 56.
29   Pocket diary, MSS-197, Box II, Folder 56. The caption says, "One of the greatest tributes ever paid Furlong by an Ona was when his principle [*sic*] Ona, Aanikin, was willing to accompany him under his promise of protection to Rio Grande ranch to secure some supplies from Estancia Sara still farther to the north. The interpreting was done by Lucas Bridges who declared that Aanikin would, under no circumstances, accompany Furlong. Lucas was astonished when Aanikin said, after it was explained, that he would go" (MSS-197, Box XII, Folder 48).
30   Derrida would have referred to these marks on Aanikin's skin as a form of "private inscription," one that leaves "the trace of an incision *right on* the skin" (*Archive Fever*, 20).
31   The Antarctica trip was part of a partnership between the Chilean Antarctic Institute and the US National Science Foundation, supported through NSF's Office of Polar Programs, award 1748137.
32   Alvarado Pérez, "Vestidura, investidura y despojo del nativo fueguino," 5. Margarita Alvarado describes Veiga as a well-known portrait photographer from Spain who opened his studio in Punta Arenas, Chile, in about 1904.
33   On this trip, Furlong was employed as a lecturer on the SS *Bleucher*, a cruise ship in the Hamburg-America line.
34   Jones, *Patagonian Panorama*, 14.
35   Bridges, *Uttermost Part of the Earth*, 125.

Lewis Henry Morgan

1. Morgan, *The American Beaver and His Works*, viii.
2. In her book *Mohawk Interruptus*, Audra Simpson examines the complexities of Morgan's relationship with Ely S. Parker, whom Morgan positioned as a kind of embodied translator of lost (pure and better) Seneca culture and traditions. Simpson argues that "American ethnology was born from the desires of each protagonist in the writing of the Iroquois past: Morgan grapples with American modernity and Parker with land losses" (85).
3. Christy Gast and I did this lecture together.
4. Morgan, *The American Beaver and His Works*, vi.
5. Morgan, *The American Beaver and His Works*, 18.
6. In "Lewis Henry Morgan," Gillian Feeley-Harnik discusses the importance of Morgan's *The American Beaver* to ideas of biosocial kinship and to contemporary multispecies ethnography.
7. Morgan, *The American Beaver and His Works*, vi.

Chapter Five. Dreamworlds of Beavers

1. Brendon Larson, an invasive species scholar, and Christopher Anderson, an ecologist who was studying the impacts of beavers in Tierra del Fuego, joined us on part of the trip.
2. Camila's approach to "undisciplined research" has been inspired by the artist Stephan Dillemuth, who describes his method as "bohemian research." See Hódi and Bogyó, "Interview with Artists Stephan Dillemuth, Maximiliane Baumgartner, Mirja Reuter, and Florian Gass."
3. This quote comes from a talk Christy and I gave at the University of Rochester, titled "Beaver Diasporas: Thinking with Lewis H. Morgan," as part of the bicentennial celebration of Morgan's life. The quote was cowritten with Camila Marambio.
4. For information about the Ensayos collective and projects, see the website https://ensayostierradelfuego.net/.
5. Camila notes that though performance can be ephemeral, it is also direct action and therefore immediately effective, though unpredictable.
6. The film *Asunto Castor* (2014) was a documentation of the performance. Staff from the *Festival de Artes Cielos del Infinito* filmed the performance.
7. In the broadest sense, *Asunto Castor* was inspired by the work of Augusto Boal, whose methodology offers both a poetics and a political rationale for using dialogic performance to engage communities on topics of pressing concern.
8. David Overend and Jamie Lorimer, who have done similar interdisciplinary work, have used the term *wild performatives* to describe events where people enact aspects of the wild with the aim of "learning to be affected" ("Wild Performatives," 529).

Traces of Derrida

1 In Gainesville, Danny Rolling killed Sonya Larsen, Christina Powell, Christina Hoyt, Tracey Paules, and Paules's roommate, Manny Taboada.
2 Fusco, "How the Art World, and Art Schools, Are Ripe for Sexual Abuse."
3 I have nothing against Derrida. If anything, I continue to be inspired by his ideas, as this book shows, and his life story. For a fascinating biography of Derrida, see Peeters, *Derrida*.

Anne Chapman

1 Chapman, "A Genealogy of My Professors and Informants."
2 My sense is that women and nonwhite anthropologists from Chapman's generation often became consigned to "area studies" rather than becoming a part of anthropology's broader history of ideas. Only scholars who work in the region know Chapman's research. For example, Taussig discusses Chapman's work in *Defacement*, and my Chilean colleagues all know her work.
3 Speculative feminism is just one of the "SF" tools that Haraway proposes are needed for multispecies storytelling and practices of companionship. Others include science fiction, science fantasy, speculative fabulation, science fact, and string figures (*Staying with the Trouble*, 10).
4 Chapman, "A Genealogy of My Professors and Informants." Luis Garibaldi Honte was a policeman and is often described as the "last Haush" living in Tierra del Fuego. Furlong corresponded with Garibaldi in 1964, during the same year that Chapman began her fieldwork with Kiepja. In the correspondence, Garibaldi says his name in Haush was "Kautel" and his mother's Spanish name was "Luisa Honten." The correspondence can be found in MSS-197, Box I, Folder 24.
5 Gabriela Álvarez Gamboa, "El texto etnográfico y la problemática indígena," discusses the ways in which Chapman's ethnographic practice aligned with standard conventions of textual holism, while also departing from these conventions, particularly in her critique of classic ethnographic accounts of Selk'nam women. In her dissertation, Camila Marambio troubles Chapman's white melancholic gaze ("Distancia," 29–53).
6 Chapman, "The End of the World." Other scholars confirm Chapman's descriptions of the rapid Fuegian genocide. European settlement brought the widespread occupation of Indigenous lands by ranchers and gold miners and vicious cycles of escalating violence, introduced diseases, and established Christian missions (Martinic B., "The Meeting of Two Cultures," 115). For discussion of the Chilean state's role in the Fuegian genocide, see Alberto Harambour and José Barrena Ruiz, "Barbarie o justicia en la Patagonia occidental."
7 Chapman, "The End of the World."
8 Chapman, *Drama and Power in a Hunting Society*.

9 Chapman, "The End of the World."
10 Thurman, "A Loss for Words."
11 Today in Chile activists are working to get Selk'nam recognition by the Chilean state. Hema'ny Molina Vargas, for example, is president of the Selk'nam Corporation Chile, formed in 2015 to maintain Selk'nam history and cultural knowledge. See Hema'ny Molina Vargas, Camila Marambio, and Nina Lykke, "Decolonising Mourning," for additional discussion.

Conclusion

Figure C.1 is from MSS-197, Box XVII, Folder 15. Figure C.2 is reproduced from a negative from MSS-197, Box XXIV, Folder 3.

1 Frank Steinheimer describes how Darwin collected the lesser rhea specimen (shot by the ship's artist, Conrad Martens) and the specimen's naming history ("Charles Darwin's Bird Collection," 308).
2 Goffinet et al., *Miniature Forests of Cape Horn*.
3 Mark Hamilton Lytle, in his examination of Carson's life and work, says that Paul Brooks, Carson's longtime editor, and Marie Rodell, her agent and friend, convinced Carson to title her manuscript *Silent Spring*, which was originally a chapter title. See Lytle, *The Gentle Subversive*, 156.
4 Andrew Whitehouse uses the term *anxious semiotics* to describe listening to birds in the Anthropocene, an experience of both pleasure and concern about their potential extinction ("Listening to Birds in the Anthropocene," 15).
5 The Yagán community, which lies a few miles east of the park in the village of Ukika, has a complex relationship with Omora. This is not surprising, as conservation and the establishment of nature parks often lead to community displacements, limitations on traditional uses of land and forest resources, and unequal local benefits. As an example, Paige West in *Conservation Is Our Government Now* demonstrates how development-based conservation efforts can transform social relations and lead to unintended environmental consequences. Moreover, communities are rarely in accord. Claudia Gonzales scolded me once, saying, "Do not speak of the *community*, only people in the community." Several respected families have worked with the Omora to document Yagán knowledge of plants, medicines, and animal life, as well as demonstrate basket making and other traditions to visitors and students. There are others in the community who feel that the "ethno" in Omora's ethno-ecological mission has led to few community benefits.
6 Brian Hochman's *Savage Preservation* provides a fascinating and thoughtful analysis of the role of photography and recordings in early anthropology. His work was helpful to my analysis here.
7 Dorsey, *The Pawnee Mythology*, xvii.
8 Letter can be found in MSS-197, Box I, Folder 36; emphasis added.

9 In a highly informative blogpost, "The Federal Cylinder Project," David Gulion describes the history of wax cylinder recorders, their use in language documentation, and the Library of Congress American Folklife Center's Federal Cylinder Project.
10 For a wonderful discussion of the trace in anthropology, which offers a model for ethnographic engagement with the materiality of the trace, see Napolitano, "Anthropology and Traces."
11 Pocket diary entry, January 8, 1908, MSS-197, Box II, Folder 57.
12 Pocket diary entry, January 9, 1908, MSS-197, Box II, Folder 57.

Bibliography

Abbott, Dorothy. "Recovering Zora Neale Hurston's Work." *Frontiers: A Journal of Women Studies* 12, no. 1 (1991): 175–81.
Abram, Simone, and Marianne Elisabeth Lien. "Performing Nature at World's Ends." *Ethnos* 76, no. 1 (2011): 3–18.
Agamben, Giorgio. "What Is an Apparatus?" In *What Is an Apparatus? And Other Essays*. Translated by David Kishik and Stefan Pedatella, 1–24. Stanford, CA: Stanford University Press, 2009.
Allentoft, Morten Erik, Rasmus Heller, Charlotte L. Oskam, Eline D. Lorenzen, Marie L. Hale, M. Thomas P. Gilbert, Christopher Jacomb, Richard N. Holdaway, and Michael Bunce. "Extinct New Zealand Megafauna Were Not in Decline before Human Colonization." *Proceedings of the National Academy of Sciences* 111, no. 13 (2014): 4922–27.
Alvarado Pérez, Margarita, Carolina Odone C., Felipa Maturana D., and Dánae Fiore, eds. *Fueguinos: Fotografías siglos XIX y XX; Imágenes e imaginarios del fin del mundo*. Santiago, Chile: Pehuén, 2013.
Alvarado Pérez, Margarita. "Vestidura, investidura y despojo del nativo fueguino: Dispositivos y procedimientos visuales en la fotografía de Tierra del Fuego (1880–1930)." In *Fueguinos: Fotografías siglos XIX y XX; Imágenes e imaginarios del fin del mundo*, edited by Margarita Alvarado P., Carolina Odone C., Felipa Maturana D. and Dánae Fiore, 7–12. Santiago, Chile: Pehuén, 2013.
Álvarez Gamboa, Gabriela. "El texto etnográfico y la problemática indígena: Las posibilidades de una escritura diferenciada en la investigación antropológica de Anne Chapman." *Atenea* 508 (2013): 91–100.
Anderson, Christopher B., Guillermo Martínez Pasture, María Vanessa Lencinas, Petra K. Wallem, Michelle C. Moorman, and Amy D. Rosemond. "Do Introduced North American Beavers *Castor canadensis* Engineer Differently in Southern South America? An Overview with Implications for Restoration." *Mammal Review* 39, no. 1 (2009): 33–52.
Armstrong, Philip. "'The Wonderment of This Taxonomy': Animals and Wonder from the Pre-modern to the Modern." In *Exploring the Animal Turn:*

Human-Animal Relations in Science, Society and Culture, edited by Erika Andersson Cederholm, Amelie Björck, Kristina Jennbert, and Ann-Sofie Lönngren, 155–70. Lund, Sweden: Lund University, 2014.

Armstrong, Richard. "Lichens, Lichenometry and Global Warming." *Microbiologist*, September 2004: 32–35.

Arnold, David. "Inventing Tropicality." In *The Problem of Nature: Environment, Culture and European Expansion*, edited by David Arnold, 141–68. Oxford: Blackwell, 1996.

Baggini, Julian. *The Pig That Wants to Be Eaten: 100 Experiments for the Armchair Philosopher*. New York: Penguin, 2006.

Ballestero, Andrea. *A Future History of Water*. Durham, NC: Duke University Press, 2019.

Barnes, David K. A., Francois Galgani, Richard C. Thompson, and Morton Barlaz. "Accumulation and Fragmentation of Plastic Debris in Global Environments." *Philosophical Transactions of the Royal Society B: Biological Sciences* 364, no. 1526 (2009): 1985–98.

Barthe, Christine. *"Uun-Daranata*: With Eyes Wide Open." In *Martin Gusinde: The Lost Tribes of Tierra del Fuego*, edited by Christine Barthes and Xavier Barral, 9–18. New York: Thames and Hudson, 2015.

Barthes, Roland. *Mourning Diary: October 26, 1977–September 15, 1979*. Edited by Natalie Léger and translated by Richard Howard. New York: Hill and Wang, 2009.

Benedict, James B. "A Review of Lichenometric Dating and Its Applications to Archaeology." *American Antiquity* 74, no. 1 (2009): 143–72.

Benjamin, Walter. "Theses on the Philosophy of History." In *Illuminations: Essays and Reflections*, edited by Hannah Arendt and translated by Harry Zohn, 253–64. New York: Schocken, 1968.

Bessire, Lucas. *Behold the Black Caiman: A Chronicle of Ayoreo Life*. Chicago: University of Chicago Press, 2014.

Brah, Avtar. *Cartographies of Diaspora: Contesting Identities*. London: Routledge, 1996.

Brandt, Annette, Jean-Pierre de Vera, Silvano Onofri, and Sieglinde Ott. "Viability of the Lichen *Xanthoria elegans* and Its Symbionts after 18 Months of Space Exposure and Simulated Mars Conditions on the ISS." *International Journal of Astrobiology* 14, no. 3 (2015): 411–25.

Breithoff, Esther, and Rodney Harrison. "From Ark to Bank: Extinction, Proxies and Biocapitals in Ex-Situ Biodiversity Conservation Practices." *International Journal of Heritage Studies* 26, no. 1 (2018): 37–55.

Bridges, E. Lucas. *Uttermost Part of the Earth*. London: Hodder and Stoughton, 1948.

Brown, Jacqueline Nassy. *Dropping Anchor, Setting Sail: Geographies of Race in Black Liverpool*. Princeton, NJ: Princeton University Press, 2005.

Brubaker, Rogers. "The 'Diaspora' Diaspora." *Ethnic and Racial Studies* 28, no. 1 (2005): 1–19.

Butland, Gilbert J. *The Human Geography of Southern Chile*. London: Institute of British Geographers, 1957.

Butler, Judith. Introduction to *Of Grammatology*, by Jacques Derrida, translated by Gayatri Chakravorty Spivak, vii–xxiv. Baltimore, MD: Johns Hopkins University Press, 2016.

Butler, Kim D. "Defining Diaspora, Refining a Discourse." *Diaspora: A Journal of Transnational Studies* 10, no. 2 (2001): 189–219.

Calloway, Colin G. *The Indian History of an American Institution: Native Americans and Dartmouth*. Hanover, NH: University Press of New England, 2010.

Cameron, Emilie. *Far Off Metal River: Inuit Lands, Settler Stories, and the Making of the Contemporary Arctic*. Vancouver: University of British Columbia Press, 2016.

Carruthers, David. "Environmental Politics in Chile: Legacies of Dictatorship and Democracy." *Third World Quarterly* 22, no. 3 (2001): 343–58.

Chapman, Anne. *Drama and Power in a Hunting Society: The Selk'nam of Tierra del Fuego*. Cambridge: Cambridge University Press, 1982.

Chapman, Anne. "The End of the World." Anne MacKaye Chapman website. Accessed December 14, 2019. http://www.thereedfoundation.org/rism/chapman/end.htm.

Chapman, Anne. *European Encounters with the Yamana People of Cape Horn, before and after Darwin*. New York: Cambridge University Press, 2010.

Chapman, Anne. "A Genealogy of My Professors and Informants." Anne MacKaye Chapman website. Accessed December 14, 2019. http://www.thereedfoundation.org/rism/chapman/genealogy.htm.

Chatwin, Bruce. *In Patagonia*. New York: Penguin Classics, 2003.

Chew, Matthew K. "Ecologists, Environmentalists, Experts, and the Invasion of the 'Second Greatest Threat.'" *International Review of Environmental History* 1 (2015): 7–26.

Chew, Matthew K., and Andrew L. Hamilton. "The Rise and Fall of Biotic Nativeness: A Historical Perspective." In *Fifty Years of Invasion Ecology: The Legacy of Charles Elton*, edited by David M. Richardson, 35–48. Oxford: Wiley-Blackwell, 2011.

Clavero, Miguel, and Emili García-Berthou. "Invasive Species Are a Leading Cause of Animal Extinctions." *Trends in Ecology and Evolution* 20, no. 3 (2005): 110.

Clifford, James. "Diasporas." *Cultural Anthropology* 9, no. 3 (1994): 302–38.

Comaroff, Jean, and John L. Comaroff. "Naturing the Nation: Aliens, Apocalypse and the Postcolonial State." *Journal of Southern African Studies* 27, no. 3 (2001): 627–51.

Cooper, John M. "Analytical and Critical Bibliography of the Tribes of Tierra del Fuego and Adjacent Territory." Washington, DC: Smithsonian Institution, Bureau of American Ethnology, 1917.

Cortesi, Luisa. "The Muddy Semiotics of Mud." *Journal of Political Ecology* 25, no. 1 (2018): 617–37.

Crosby, Alfred W. *Ecological Imperialism: The Biological Expansion of Europe, 900-1900.* 2nd ed. Cambridge: Cambridge University Press, 2004.

Darwin, Charles. *The Autobiography of Charles Darwin: 1809-1882.* Edited with appendix and notes by Nora Barlow. London: Collins, 1958. http://darwin-online.org.uk/content/frameset?itemID=F1497&viewtype=text&pageseq=1.

Darwin, Charles. *Journal of Researches into the Natural History and Geology of the Countries Visited during the Voyage of H.M.S. Beagle round the World, under the Command of Capt. Fitz Roy.* 2nd ed. London: John Murray, 1845.

Davis, Heather, and Zoe Todd. "On the Importance of a Date, or Decolonizing the Anthropocene." *ACME* 16, no. 4 (2017): 761-80.

Davis, Mark A., et al. "Don't Judge Species on Their Origins." *Nature* 474 (June 9, 2011): 153-54.

Davis, Susan E., and Margo DeMello. *Stories Rabbits Tell: A Natural and Cultural History of a Misunderstood Creature.* New York: Lantern Books, 2003.

de la Cadena, Marisol. *Earth Beings: Ecologies of Practice across Andean Worlds.* Durham, NC: Duke University Press, 2015.

de la Cadena, Marisol. "Uncommons." *Theorizing the Contemporary, Cultural Anthropology* (blog), March 29, 2018. https://culanth.org/fieldsights/uncommons.

Deloria, Philip J. *Playing Indian.* New Haven, CT: Yale University Press, 1999.

Derrida, Jacques. *Archive Fever: A Freudian Impression.* Translated by Eric Prenowitz. Chicago: University of Chicago Press, 1996.

Di Giminiani, Piergiorgio. *Sentient Lands: Indigeneity, Property, and Political Imagination in Neoliberal Chile.* Tucson: University of Arizona Press, 2018.

Dorsey, George Amos. *The Pawnee Mythology.* Lincoln: University of Nebraska Press, 1997.

Ellis, Erle C. *Anthropocene: A Very Short Introduction.* Oxford: Oxford University Press, 2018.

Escobar, Arturo. *Designs for the Pluriverse: Radical Interdependence, Autonomy, and the Making of Worlds.* Durham, NC: Duke University Press, 2018.

Escobar, Arturo. *Territories of Difference: Place, Movements, Life, Redes.* Durham, NC: Duke University Press, 2008.

Feeley-Harnik, Gillian. "Lewis Henry Morgan: American Beavers and Their Works." *Ethnos* 86, no. 1 (2021): 21-43. https://doi.org/10.1080/00141844.2019.1619605.

Finkelstein, Maura. *The Archive of Loss: Lively Ruination in Mill Land Mumbai.* Durham, NC: Duke University Press, 2019.

Flusser, Vilém, and Louis Bec. *Vampyroteuthis infernalis: A Treatise, with a Report by the Institut Scientifique de Recherche Paranaturaliste.* Minneapolis: University of Minnesota Press, 2012.

Fraser, Crystal, and Zoe Todd. "Decolonial Sensibilities: Indigenous Research and Engaging with Archives in Contemporary Colonial Canada." In *Decolonising Archives*, 32-39. L'Internationale Books, 2016. https://www

.internationaleonline.org/research/decolonising_practices/54_decolonial _sensibilities_indigenous_research_and_engaging_with_archives_in _contemporary_colonial_canada.

Fudge, Erica. *Animal*. London: Reaktion, 2002.

Furlong, Charles Wellington. "The Alaculoofs and Yahgans, the World's Southernmost Inhabitants." In *Proceedings of the Nineteenth International Congress of Americanists*, edited by F. W. Hodge, 224-34. Washington, DC: ICA Press, 1917.

Furlong, Charles Wellington. "Amid the Islands of the Land of Fire." *Harper's Magazine* 118, no. 716 (1909): 335-47.

Furlong, Charles Wellington. "Brief Notes on the Furlong Collections." *American Anthropologist* 67, no. 2 (1965): 462-69.

Furlong, Charles Wellington. "Exploration in Tierra del Fuego and the Fuegian Archipelago." *Geographical Journal* 81, no. 3 (1933): 211-24.

Furlong, Charles Wellington. "Into the Unknown Land of the Onas." *Harper's Magazine* 119, no. 711 (1909): 443-55.

Furlong, Charles Wellington. Papers of Charles Wellington Furlong, Stefansson Collection, Rauner Special Collections Library, Dartmouth College, Dartmouth, NH.

Furlong, Charles Wellington. "Some Effects of Environment on the Fuegian Tribes." *Geographical Review* 3, no. 1 (1917): 1-15.

Furlong, Charles Wellington. "The Southernmost People in the World." *Harper's Magazine* 119, no. 709 (1909): 126-37.

Furlong, Charles Wellington. "The Vanishing People of the Land of Fire." *Harper's Magazine* 120, no. 716 (1910): 217-28.

Fusco, Coco. "How the Art World, and Art Schools, Are Ripe for Sexual Abuse." *Hyperallergic* (blog), November 14, 2017. https://hyperallergic.com/411343 /how-the-art-world-and-art-schools-are-ripe-for-sexual-abuse/.

Galloway, David J. "Phytogeography of Southern Hemisphere Lichens." In *Quantitative Approaches to Phytogeography*, edited by Pier Luigi Nimis and T. J. Crovello, 233-62. New York: Springer, 1991.

Galton, Francis. *Finger Prints*. London: Macmillan, 1892.

García O., Samuel. "Vestigios patrimoniales del aserradero Caleta María, Tierra del Fuego (Chile)." *Magallania (Chile)* 41, no. 1 (2013): 53-82.

Ghosh, Amitav. *The Great Derangement: Climate Change and the Unthinkable*. Berlin Family Lectures. Chicago: University of Chicago Press, 2017.

Gilroy, Paul. "Cultural Studies and Ethnic Absolutism." In *Cultural Studies*, edited by Lawrence Grossberg, Cary Nelson, and Paula Treichler, 187-99. London: Routledge, 1992.

Gilroy, Paul. *"There Ain't No Black in the Union Jack": The Cultural Politics of Race and Nation*. London: Hutchinson, 1987.

Ginn, William J. *Investing in Nature: Case Studies of Land Conservation in Collaboration with Business*. Washington, DC: Island Press, 2005.

Ginzburg, Carlo. "Clues: Roots of an Evidential Paradigm." In *Clues, Myths, and the Historical Method*, translated by John Tedeschi and Anne C. Tedeschi, 87–113. Baltimore, MD: Johns Hopkins University Press, 1989.

Goffinet, Bernard, Ricardo Rozzi, Lily Lewis, William Buck, and Francisca Massardo. *Miniature Forests of Cape Horn: Ecotourism with a Hand Lens*. Bilingual ed. Denton: University of North Texas Press, 2012.

Gonzalez Poblete, Exequiel, Benjamin M. Drakeford, Felipe Hurtado Ferreira, Makarena Garrido Barraza, and Pierre Failler. "The Impact of Trade and Markets on Chilean Atlantic Salmon Farming." *Aquaculture International* 27, no. 5 (2019): 1465–83.

Greenblatt, Stephen. *Marvelous Possessions: The Wonder of the New World*. Chicago: University of Chicago Press, 1992.

Gruber, Jacob W. "Ethnographic Salvage and the Shaping of Anthropology." *American Anthropologist* 72 (1970): 1289–99.

Gulion, David. "The Federal Cylinder Project: Preservation of a Fragile Collection." *Reading, Writing, Research* (blog), May 16, 2018. https://www.all purposeguru.com/2018/05/the-federal-cylinder-project-preservation-of -a-fragile-collection/.

Gusinde, Martin. "Zentral-Amerika und Südamerika." *Ethnologischer Anzeiger* 2 (1929): 43–79.

Hadfield, Michael G., and Donna J. Haraway. "The Tree Snail Manifesto." *Current Anthropology* 60, no. S20 (2019): S209–35.

Hall, Stuart. "Culture Identity and Diaspora." In *Identity: Community, Culture, Difference*, edited by Jonathon Rutherford, 222–37. London: Lawrence and Wishart, 1990.

Harambour, Alberto, and José Barrena Ruiz. "Barbarie o justicia en la Patagonia occidental: Las violencias coloniales en el ocaso del pueblo Kawésqa, finales del siglo XIX e inicios del siglo XX." *Historia Crítica* 71 (2019): 25–48.

Haraway, Donna J. *Staying with the Trouble: Making Kin in the Chthulucene*. Durham, NC: Duke University Press, 2016.

Haraway, Donna. "Teddy Bear Patriarchy: Taxidermy in the Garden of Eden, New York City, 1908-1936." *Social Text* 11 (1984): 20–64.

Haraway, Donna J. *When Species Meet*. Minneapolis: University of Minnesota, 2008.

Hartigan, John. "Mexican Genomics and the Roots of Racial Thinking." *Cultural Anthropology* 28, no. 3 (2013): 372–95.

Hazlewood, Nick. *Savage: The Life and Times of Jemmy Button*. New York: Thomas Dunne Books, 2001.

Heatherington, Tracey. "Seeds." *Theorizing the Contemporary, Cultural Anthropology* (blog), June 28, 2017. https://culanth.org/fieldsights/seeds ?token=ht6b9tmcw_soswaqhq7ihi-4rwf37mec.

Hintzen, Percy C., and Jean Muteba Rahier. "Introduction: Theorizing the African Diaspora: Metaphor, Misrecognition, and Self-Recognition." In *Global Circuits of Blackness: Interrogating the African Diaspora*, edited by Jean Muteba

Rahier, Percy C. Hintzen, and Felipe Smith, ix–xxvi. Champaign: University of Illinois Press, 2010.

Hochman, Brian. *Savage Preservation: The Ethnographic Origins of Modern Media Technology.* Minneapolis: University of Minnesota Press, 2014.

Hódi, Csilla, and Virág Bogyó. "Interview with Artists Stephan Dillemuth, Maximiliane Baumgartner, Mirja Reuter, and Florian Gass." *Tranzit.* Accessed December 15, 2019. http://tranzit.org/file/PR_group_Stephan_Dillemuth_e.pdf.

Holling, C. S., and Gary K. Meffe. "Command and Control and the Pathology of Natural Resource Management." *Conservation Biology* 10, no. 2 (1996): 328–37.

Houck, Oliver A. *Taking Back Eden: Eight Environmental Cases That Changed the World.* Washington, DC: Island Press, 2010.

Hurston, Zora Neale. "Florida's Migrant Farm Labor." *Frontiers: A Journal of Women's Studies* 12, no. 1 (1991): 199–205.

Jaksic, Fabián M., and Jose R. Yañez. "Rabbit and Fox Introductions in Tierra del Fuego: History and Assessment of the Attempts at Biological Control of the Rabbit Infestation." *Biological Conservation* 26 (1983): 367–74.

Jansen, Bart. "Massive Iceberg Looms off Greenland Coast, Threatening Tiny Village." *USA Today,* July 13, 2018.

Jantz, Richard L. "Anthropological Dermatoglyphic Research." *Annual Review of Anthropology* 16 (1987): 161–77.

Jarvis, Brooke. "The Obsessive Search for the Tasmanian Tiger." *New Yorker,* June 25, 2018. https://www.newyorker.com/magazine/2018/07/02/the-obsessive-search-for-the-tasmanian-tiger.

Jones, Tom P. *Patagonian Panorama.* London: Outspoken Press, 1961.

Klepeis, Peter, and Paul Laris. "Contesting Sustainable Development in Tierra del Fuego." *Geoforum* 37 (2006): 505–18.

Klepeis, Peter, and Paul Laris. "Hobby Ranching and Chile's Land-Reform Legacy." *Geographical Review* 98, no. 3 (2008): 372–94.

Klubock, Thomas Miller. "The Politics of Forests and Forestry on Chile's Southern Frontier, 1880–1940s." *Hispanic American Historical Review* 86, no. 3 (2006): 535–70.

Knoblauch, Jessica A. "The Environmental Toll of Plastics." *Environmental Health News* (blog), October 26, 2017. https://www.ehn.org/plastic-environmental-impact-2501923191.html.

Kolbert, Elizabeth. *The Sixth Extinction: An Unnatural History.* New York: Henry Holt, 2014.

Larson, Brendon. "The War of the Roses: Demilitarizing Invasion Biology." *Frontiers in Ecology and the Environment* 3, no. 9 (2005): 495–500.

Leakey, Mary D. "Footprints in the Ashes of Time." *National Geographic* 155, no. 4 (1979): 446–57.

Legoupil, Dominique. "The Population and Depopulation of Tierra del Fuego."

In *Martin Gusinde: The Lost Tribes of Tierra del Fuego*, edited by Christine Barthes and Xavier Barral, 285–91. New York: Thames and Hudson, 2015.

Lepselter, Susan. *The Resonance of Unseen Things: Poetics, Power, Captivity, and UFOs in the American Uncanny*. Ann Arbor: University of Michigan Press, 2016.

Lewis, Simon L., and Mark A. Maslin. "Defining the Anthropocene." *Nature* 519 (2015): 171–80.

Li, Tania Murray. "Territory, Belonging and the Work of Inscription on an Indigenous Land Frontier." Paper presented at the American Anthropological Association meetings, Washington, DC, 2014.

Lidström, Susanna, Simon West, Tania Katzschner, M. Isabel Pérez-Ramos, and Hedley Twidle. "Invasive Narratives and the Inverse of Slow Violence: Alien Species in Science and Society." *Environmental Humanities* 7, no. 1 (2016): 1–40.

Lien, Marianne Elisabeth, and John Law. "'Emergent Aliens': On Salmon, Nature, and Their Enactment." *Ethnos* 76, no. 1 (2011): 65–87.

Lliboutry, Louis. "Glaciers of Chile and Argentina." In *Satellite Image Atlas of Glaciers of the World: South America*. US Geological Survey, Professional Paper 1386-I. Washington, DC: US Government Printing Office, 1998.

Lopez, Patricia J., and Kathryn A. Gillespie, eds. *Economies of Death: Economic Logics of Killable Life and Grievable Death*. New York: Routledge, 2015.

Luciano, Dana. "The Inhuman Anthropocene." *Avidly* (blog), March 22, 2015. http://avidly.lareviewofbooks.org/2015/03/22/the-inhuman-anthropocene.

Lytle, Mark Hamilton. *The Gentle Subversive: Rachel Carson, Silent Spring, and the Rise of the Environmental Movement*. New York: Oxford University Press, 2007.

Marambio, Camila. "Distancia: A Measure of Intimacy." PhD diss., Monash University, 2019.

Martinic Beros, Mateo. "El acervo patrimonial de Tierra del Fuego." In *Fueguinos: Fotografías siglos XIX y XX; Imágenes e imaginarios del fin del mundo*, 2nd ed., edited by Margarita Álvarado P., Carolina Odone C., Felipe Maturana D., and Dánae Fiore, 13–14. Santiago de Chile: Pehuén, 2013.

Martinic Beros, Mateo. "The Meeting of Two Cultures: Indians and Colonists in the Magellan Region." In *Patagonia: Natural History, Prehistory, and Ethnography at the Uttermost End of the Earth*, edited by Colin McEwan, Luis A. Borrero, and Alfredo Prieto, 110–26. Durham, NC: Duke University Press, 1997.

Martinic Beros, Mateo. "Recordando a un imperio pastoral: La sociedad explotadora de Tierra del Fuego (1893–1973)." *Magallania (Punta Arenas)* 39 (2011): 5–32.

Maturana Díaz, Felipe A. "Fotografía antropológica de Charles Wellington Furlong (Archipiélago Fueguino, 1907–1908)." *Revista chilena de antropología visual* 6 (December 2005): 74–94.

Mavalwala, Janshed. "A Note on the Dermatoglyphics of the Ona and Yahgan of Tierra del Fuego." *Man*, January–February 1964: 5–6.

Maxwell, H. S., and M. F. Gardner. "The Quest for Chilean Green Treasure:

Some Notable British Collectors before 1940." *New Plantsman* 4, no. 4 (1997): 199.

Mbembe, Achille. *On the Postcolony*. Berkeley: University of California Press, 2001.

Mendoza, Marcos. *The Patagonian Sublime: The Green Economy and Post-neoliberal Politics*. New Brunswick, NJ: Rutgers University Press, 2018.

Mendoza, Marcos, Robert Fletcher, George Holmes, Laura A. Ogden, and Colombina Schaeffer. "The Patagonian Imaginary: Natural Resources and Global Capitalism at the Far End of the World." *Journal of Latin American Geography* 16, no. 2 (2017): 93–116.

Miller, J. Hillis. "Trace (OG 47, 65, 66–7, 70–1; DG 69, 95, 97, 102–4)." In *Reading Derrida's "Of Grammatology,"* edited by Sean Gaston and Ian Maclachlan, 47–49. London: Continuum International, 2011.

Molina Vargas, Hema'ny, Camila Marambio, and Nina Lykke. "Decolonising Mourning: World-Making with the Selk'nam People of Karokynka/Tierra del Fuego." *Australian Feminist Studies* 35, no. 104 (2020): 186–201.

Morgan, Lewis Henry. *The American Beaver and His Works*. Philadelphia: J. B. Lippincott, 1868.

Morgan, Lewis H. *Ancient Society or Researches in the Lines of Human Progress from Savagery through Barbarism to Civilization*. London: Macmillan, 1877.

Napolitano, Valentina. "Anthropology and Traces." *Anthropological Theory* 15, no. 1 (2014): 47–67.

Nuwer, Rachel. "Lichens Do Not Age." *Smithsonian*, January 2, 2013. https://www.smithsonianmag.com/smart-news/lichens-do-not-age-120852/.

Ogden, Laura A. "The Beaver Diaspora: A Thought Experiment." *Environmental Humanities* 10, no. 1 (2018): 63–85.

Ogden, Laura A. "Saturate." In *Veer Ecology: A Companion for Environmental Thinking*, edited by Jeffrey Jerome Cohen and Lowell Duckert, 297–311. Minneapolis: University of Minnesota Press, 2017.

Ogden, Laura A. *Swamplife: People, Gators, and Mangroves Entangled in the Everglades*. Minneapolis: University of Minnesota Press, 2011.

Overend, David, and Jamie Lorimer. "Wild Performatives: Experiments in Rewilding at the Knepp Wildland Project." *GeoHumanities* 4, no. 2 (2018): 527–42.

Palma Behnke, Marisol. "Diario del primer viaje de Martín Gusinde a Tierra del Fuego (1918–1919)." *Anthropos* 113, no. 1 (2018): 169–94.

Palma Behnke, Marisol. "Diario del segundo viaje de Martín Gusinde a Fuego Patagonia (1919–1920): Introducción y comentario a la publicación del documento inédito." *Anthropos* 113, no. 2 (2018): 543–72.

Palma Behnke, Marisol. "'To Save What Is Left': Martin Gusinde in Tierra del Fuego 1918–1924." In *Martin Gusinde: The Lost Tribes of Tierra del Fuego*, edited by Christine Barthes and Xavier Barral, 19–27. New York: Thames and Hudson, 2015.

Patagon Journal. "The Yagan's Letter to the King of Norway: 'Don't Install This Destructive Industry in Our Territory.'" April 5, 2019. http://www

.patagonjournal.com/index.php?option=com_content&view=article&id =4207%3Ala-carta-de-la-comunidad-yagan-a-los-reyes-de-noruega-no -instalen-esta-industria-destructiva-en-nuestro-territorio&catid=60%3 Aeditor&Itemid=264&lang=en.

Peeters, Benoît. *Derrida: A Biography*. Translated by Andrew Brown. Cambridge: Polity, 2010.

Petrigh, Romina S., and Martín H. Fugassa. "Molecular Identification of a Fuegian Dog Belonging to the Fagnano Regional Museum Ethnographic Collection, Tierra del Fuego." *Quaternary in South America: Recent Research Initiatives* 317 (December 2013): 14–18.

Pietrek, Alejandro G., and Laura Fasola. "Origin and History of the Beaver Introduction in South America." *Mastozoología Neotropical* 21, no. 2 (2014): 355–59.

Pietrek, Alejandro G., and Mariano González-Roglich. "Post-establishment Changes in Habitat Selection by an Invasive Species: Beavers in the Patagonian Steppe." *Biological Invasions* 17, no. 11 (2015): 3225–35.

Pike, Sarah M. *For the Wild: Ritual and Commitment in Radical Eco-Activism*. Berkeley: University of California Press, 2017.

Plitt, Charles C. "A Short History of Lichenology." *Bryologist* 22, no. 6 (1919): 77–85.

Plumwood, Val. "Being Prey." In *The Ultimate Journey: Inspiring Stories of Living and Dying*, edited by James O'Reilly, Sean O'Reilly, and Richard Sterling, 128–46. San Francisco: Travelers' Tales, 1999.

Povinelli, Elizabeth A. *Geontologies: A Requiem to Late Liberalism*. Durham, NC: Duke University Press, 2016.

Pratt, Mary Louise. *Imperial Eyes: Travel Writing and Transculturation*. London: Routledge, 1992.

Pringle, Anne. "Establishing New Worlds: The Lichens of Petersham." In *Arts of Living on a Damaged Planet: Ghosts and Monsters of the Anthropocene*, edited by Anna Lowenhaupt Tsing, Nils Bubandt, Elaine Gan, and Heather Anne Swanson, G157–67. Minneapolis: University of Minnesota Press, 2017.

Prothero, Donald R. *Bringing Fossils to Life: An Introduction to Paleobiology*. 2nd ed. New York: McGraw-Hill, 2004.

Quiñones, Renato A., Marcelo Fuentes, Rodrigo M. Montes, Doris Soto, and Jorge León-Muñoz. "Environmental Issues in Chilean Salmon Farming: A Review." *Reviews in Aquaculture* 11, no. 2 (2019): 375–402.

Raffles, Hugh. "Mother Nature's Melting Pot." *New York Times*, April 3, 2011.

Rahier, Jean Muteba. "Blackness, the Racial/Spatial Order, Migrations, and Miss Ecuador 1995–96." *American Anthropologist* 100 (1998): 421–30.

Reo, Nicholas J., and Laura A. Ogden. "Anishnaabe Aki: An Indigenous Perspective on the Global Threat of Invasive Species." *Sustainability Science* 13, no. 5 (2018): 1443–52.

Rich, Nathaniel. "Losing Earth: The Decade We Almost Stopped Climate Change." *New York Times Magazine*, August 1, 2018.

Robbins, Paul, and Sarah A. Moore. "Ecological Anxiety Disorder: Diagnosing the Politics of the Anthropocene." *Cultural Geographies* 20, no. 1 (2013): 3–19.

Rojas W., Alejandro, Francisco Sabatini, and Claudia Sepúlveda. "Conflictos ambientales en Chile: Aprendizajes y desafíos." *Revista Ambiente y Desarrollo* 21, no. 3 (2003): 22–30.

Rosaldo, Renato. "Imperialist Nostalgia." *Representations* 26 (Spring 1989): 107–22.

Royle, S. A. "Exploration." In *International Encyclopedia of Human Geography*, edited by Rob Kitchin and Nigel Thrift, 676–82. Oxford: Elsevier, 2009.

Rozzi, Ricardo, and Kurt Heidinger. *The Route of Darwin through the Cape Horn Archipelago*. Punta Arenas, Chile: Gobierno Regional de Magallanes y Antártica Chilena, 2006.

Rubenstein, Mary-Jane. *Strange Wonder: The Closure of Metaphysics and the Opening of Awe*. New York: Columbia University Press, 2008.

Ruppel, Richard. "Pathos and Fun: Conrad and *Harper's Magazine*." *Conradiana* 41, no. 2 (2009): 178–200.

Sala, Osvaldo E., F. Stuart Chapin III, Juan J. Armesto, Eric Berlow, Janine Bloomfield, Rodolfo Dirzo, et al. "Global Biodiversity Scenarios for the Year 2100." *Science* 287, no. 5459 (2000): 1770–74.

Sancho, Leopoldo. "Lichens and Their Habitats at the Omora Ethnobotanical Park and Navarino Island." In *Miniature Forests of Cape Horn: Ecotourism with a Hand Lens*, edited by Bernard Goffinet, Ricardo Rozzi, Lily Lewis, William Buck, and Francisca Massardo, 154–70. Denton: University of North Texas Press, 2012.

Satterfield, Terre. *Anatomy of a Conflict: Identity, Knowledge, and Emotion in Old-Growth Forests*. Vancouver: University of British Columbia Press, 2002.

Schlaepfer, M. A., D. F. Sax, and J. D. Olden. "The Potential Conservation Value of Non-native Species." *Conservation Biology* 25, no. 3 (2011): 428–37.

Seigworth, Gregory J., and Melissa Gregg. "An Inventory of Shimmers." In *The Affect Theory Reader*, edited by Melissa Gregg and Gregory J. Seigworth, 1–25. Durham, NC: Duke University Press, 2010.

Sepúlveda, Claudia, and Pablo Villarroel. "Swans, Conflicts, and Resonance: Local Movements and the Reform of Chilean Environmental Institutions." *Latin American Perspectives* 39, no. 4 (2012): 181–200.

Serres, Michael. *Conversations on Science, Culture, and Time*. Translated by Roxanne Lapidus. Ann Arbor: University of Michigan Press, 1995.

Sherwood, Dave. "Chile Regulator Charges Marine Harvest with Environmental Breaches." *Reuters*, October 31, 2018. https://www.reuters.com/article/us-chile-salmon/chile-regulator-charges-marine-harvest-with-environmental-breaches-idUSKCN1N52LR.

Silva, Claudia A., and Bárbara Saavedra. "Knowing for Controlling: Ecological Effects of Invasive Vertebrates in Tierra del Fuego." *Revista Chilena de Historia Natural* 81, no. 1 (2008): 123–36.

Simberloff, Daniel, Jake Alexander, Fred Allendorf, James Aronson, Pedro M.

Anunes, Sven Bacher, Richard Bardgett, et al. "Non-natives: 141 Scientists Object." *Nature* 475, no. 7354 (2011): 1.

Simberloff, Daniel, Jean-Louis Martin, Piero Genovesi, Virginie Maris, David A. Wardle, James Aronson, Franck Courchamp, et al. "Impacts of Biological Invasions: What's What and the Way Forward." *Trends in Ecology and Evolution* 28, no. 1 (2013): 58–66.

Simpson, Audra. *Mohawk Interruptus: Political Life across the Borders of Settler States*. Durham, NC: Duke University Press, 2014.

Smith, Bruce D., and Melinda A. Zeder. "The Onset of the Anthropocene." *Anthropocene* 4 (2013): 8–13.

Snow, W. Parker. "A Few Remarks on the Wild Tribes of Tierra del Fuego from Personal Observation." *Transactions of the Ethnological Society of London* 1 (1861): 261–67.

Solnit, Rebecca. *Hope in the Dark: Untold Histories, Wild Possibilities*. 3rd ed. Chicago: Haymarket Books, 2016.

Soluri, John. "Something Fishy: Chile's Blue Revolution, Commodity Diseases, and the Problem of Sustainability." *Latin American Research Review* 46 (2011): 55–81.

Srinivas, Tulasi. *The Cow in the Elevator: An Anthropology of Wonder*. Durham, NC: Duke University Press, 2018.

Steffen, Will, Wendy Broadgate, Lisa Deutsch, Owen Gaffney, and Cornelia Ludwig. "The Trajectory of the Anthropocene: The Great Acceleration." *Anthropocene Review* 2, no. 1 (2015): 81–98.

Steffen, Will, Paul J. Crutzen, and John R. McNeill. "The Anthropocene: Are Humans Now Overwhelming the Great Forces of Nature." *AMBIO: A Journal of the Human Environment* 36, no. 8 (2007): 614–21.

Steinheimer, Frank D. "Charles Darwin's Bird Collection and Ornithological Knowledge during the Voyage of H.M.S. 'Beagle,' 1831–1836." *Journal of Ornithology* 145, no. 4 (2004): 300–320.

Stengers, Isabelle. *Cosmopolitics I*. Translated by Robert Bonnono. Minneapolis: University of Minnesota Press, 2010.

Stengers, Isabelle. "Diderot's Egg: Divorcing Materialism from Eliminativism." *Radical Philosophy* 144 (2007): 7–15.

Stengers, Isabelle. "Including Nonhumans in Political Theory: Opening Pandora's Box?" In *Political Matter: Technoscience, Democracy, and Public Life*, edited by Bruce Braun and Sarah J. Whatmore, 3–31. Minneapolis: University of Minnesota Press, 2010.

Stengers, Isabelle. "Wondering about Materialism." In *The Speculative Turn: Continental Materialism and Realism*, edited by Levi Bryant, Nick Srnicek, and Graham Harman, 368–80. Melbourne: re.press, 2011.

Stewart, Kathleen. *Ordinary Affects*. Durham, NC: Duke University Press, 2007.

Stocking, George W., Jr. "Colonial Situations." In *Colonial Situations: Essays on the Contextualization of Ethnographic Knowledge*, edited by George W. Stocking Jr., 3–7. Madison: University of Wisconsin Press, 1991.

Stoler, Ann Laura. *Along the Archival Grain: Epistemic Anxieties and Colonial Common Sense*. Princeton, NJ: Princeton University Press, 2009.

Sturm, Circe. *Blood Politics: Race, Culture, and Identity in the Cherokee Nation of Oklahoma*. Berkeley: University of California Press, 2002.

Subramaniam, Banu. "The Aliens Have Landed! Reflections on the Rhetoric of Biological Invasions." *Meridians* 2, no. 1 (2001): 26–40.

Swanson, Heather Anne, Marianne Elisabeth Lien, and Gro B. Ween, eds. *Domestication Gone Wild: Politics and Practices of Multispecies Relations*. Durham, NC: Duke University Press, 2018.

TallBear, Kim. "Beyond the Life/Not-Life Binary: A Feminist-Indigenous Reading of Cryopreservation, Interspecies Thinking, and the New Materialisms." In *Cryopolitics: Frozen Life in a Melting World*, edited by Joanna Radin and Emma Kowal, 179–202. Cambridge, MA: MIT Press, 2017.

TallBear, Kim. *Native American DNA: Tribal Belonging and the False Promise of Genetic Science*. Minneapolis: University of Minnesota Press, 2013.

Taussig, Michael. *Defacement: Public Secrecy and the Labor of the Negative*. Stanford, CA: Stanford University Press, 1999.

Taussig, Michael. *Fieldwork Notebooks: 100 Notes, 100 Thoughts*. Vol. 1. Documenta Series 13. Berlin: Hatje Cantz Verlag, 2011.

Taussig, Michael. *Mimesis and Alterity: A Particular History of the Senses*. New York: Routledge, 1993.

Tecklin, David, Carl Bauer, and Manuel Prieto. "Making Environmental Law for the Market: The Emergence, Character, and Implications of Chile's Environmental Regime." *Environmental Politics* 20, no. 6 (2011): 879–98.

Thomas, Chris D., Alison Cameron, Rhys E. Green, Michel Bakkenes, Linda J. Beaumont, Yvonne C. Collingham, Barend F. N. Erasmus, et al. "Extinction Risk from Climate Change." *Nature* 427, no. 6970 (2004): 145–48.

Thurman, Judith. "A Loss for Words: Can a Dying Language Be Saved?" *New Yorker*, March 30, 2015. https://www.newyorker.com/magazine/2015/03/30/a-loss-for-words.

Tsing, Anna Lowenhaupt. *The Mushroom at the End of the World: On the Possibility of Life in Capitalist Ruins*. Princeton, NJ: Princeton University Press, 2015.

Tsing, Anna L. "On Nonscalability: The Living World Is Not Amenable to Precision-Nested Scales." *Common Knowledge* 18, no. 3 (2014): 505–24.

Tsing, Anna Lowenhaupt, Andrew S. Mathews, and Nils Bubandt. "Patchy Anthropocene: Landscape Structure, Multispecies History, and the Retooling of Anthropology." *Current Anthropology* 60, no. S20 (2019): S186–97.

Tsing, Anna Lowenhaupt, Heather Anne Swanson, Elaine Gan, and Nils Bubandt, eds. *Arts of Living on a Damaged Planet: Ghosts and Monsters of the Anthropocene*. Minneapolis: University of Minnesota Press, 2017.

Tuck, Eve, and Wayne K. Yang. "Decolonization Is Not a Metaphor." *Decolonization: Indigeneity, Education and Society* 1, no. 1 (2012): 1–40.

van Dooren, Thom. *Flight Ways: Life and Loss at the Edge of Extinction*. New York: Columbia University Press, 2014.

Venn, Couze. "Identity, Diasporas, and Subjective Change: The Role of Affect, the Relation to the Other, and the Aesthetic." *Subjectivity* 26 (2009): 3–28.

Vitousek, Peter M., Carla M. D'Antonio, Lloyd L. Loope, and Randy Westbrooks. "Biological Invasions as Global Environmental Change." *American Scientist* 84, no. 5 (1996): 218–28.

Waters, Colin N., Jan Zalasiewicz, Colin Summerhayes, Anthony D. Barnosky, Clément Poirier, Agnieszka Gałuszka, Alejandro Cearreta, et al. "The Anthropocene Is Functionally and Stratigraphically Distinct from the Holocene." *Science* 351, no. 6269 (2016). https://doi.org/10.1126/science.aAD2622.

West, Paige. *Conservation Is Our Government Now: The Politics of Ecology in Papua New Guinea*. Durham, NC: Duke University Press, 2006.

West, Paige. *Dispossession and the Environment: Rhetoric and Inequality in Papua New Guinea*. New York: Columbia University Press, 2016.

Whidbey Environmental Action Network. "WEAN's History with Trillium Corp." Accessed May 1, 2020. https://www.whidbeyenvironment.org/history-with-trillium.

Whitehouse, Andrew. "Listening to Birds in the Anthropocene: The Anxious Semiotics of Sound in a Human-Dominated World." *Environmental Humanities* 6 (2015): 53–71.

Whyte, Kyle P. "Indigenous Science (Fiction) for the Anthropocene: Ancestral Dystopias and Fantasies of Climate Change Crises." *Environment and Planning E: Nature and Space* 1, nos. 1–2 (2018): 224–42.

Wolfe, Patrick. "Settler Colonialism and the Elimination of the Native." *Journal of Genocide Research* 8, no. 4 (2006): 387–409.

Yong, Ed. "The Overlooked Organisms That Keep Challenging Our Assumptions about Life." *Atlantic*, January 17, 2019.

Yusoff, Kathryn. *A Billion Black Anthropocenes or None*. Minneapolis: University of Minnesota Press, 2018.

Zalasiewicz, Jan, Colin N. Waters, Juliana A. Ivar do Sul, Patricia L. Corcoran, Anthony D. Barnosky, Alejandro Cearreta, Matt Edgeworth, et al. "The Geological Cycle of Plastics and Their Use as a Stratigraphic Indicator of the Anthropocene." *Anthropocene* 13, supplement C (2016): 4–17.

Zand, Tristan. "An Introduction to Dualphotography." *Medium* (blog), April 8, 2017. https://medium.com/dualphoto/an-introduction-to-dual photography-b17f02049bbf.

Index

Italic *f*s following page numbers refer to figures.

Aanikin, 22*f*, 23, 87, 89*f*, 96*f*, 100–103, 101*f*, 103*f*, 138–40, 164nn29–30
Abram, Simone, 146n7
Agamben, Giorgio, 99, 145n5
agrarian reform, 79
Alday, David, 54–56, 55*f*
Allen Gardiner Massacre, 35–40
American Beaver and His Works, The (Morgan), 108–10
Antarctica: Chilean research station, 104; Larsen C, 5, 6; plastics and the Anthropocene in, 49; tourists on the way to, 8, 113
Anthropocene, 48–49, 152nn1–2, 152n5, 153n10, 154n14, 167n4
apparatuses: Agamben on, 99, 145n5; beaver skin trade, 67–68; of colonialism, 17, 32; defined, 145n5; figures and, 2–3; Furlong's subject position and, 99; introduction of plant and animal life, 84; loss, wonder, and, 134; photography and, 106; sheep complex, 76; World's End, 99. *See also* entanglements; inscription practices
archives: decolonization and, 42–43; Derrida on, 16, 52–53, 148n1; earth, archival, 38–43, 47–50; evidence of the present, 12; Furlong's archival self, 16–20; nontraditional sites and, 148n21; origins, forgetting of, 53; proliferation of, 106; structuring logic of, 12, 147n20. *See also* Furlong Papers, Dartmouth College
Arnold, David, 146n7
Asunto Castor (Gast and Marambio), 119–20, 120*f*, 124, 165nn6–7

baguales (domesticated animals "gone wild"), 81
Balance, Laura, 127*f*, 129
Ballestero, Andrea, 146n6
Barthes, Roland, 5, 128
Basket, Fuegia, 28, 40
Beagle, HMS, 28–29
Beagle Channel, 29*f*, 57*f*; beaver in, 67; map, 32*f*; Picton Island, 84; salmon farming and Yagán claims to, 54
Beaver Dance (film), 123–24
beavers, 62*f*; anthropology and, 108–10; *Asunto Castor* (film and performance), 119–20, 120*f*, 124, 165nn6–7; beaver dam sketch (Colloredo-Mansfeld), 107*f*; *Beaver Dance* (film), 123–24; *Castorera (A Love Story)* (film), 125–26, 125*f*; costumes, human-size, 118–26; as diaspora, 66–67, 84; *Dreamworlds of Beavers*, 111*f*, 112–13; forest beavers, 69–75; introduction of, 63, 68; invasive species paradigm and, 64–69; killability and, 63–65;

beavers (*continued*)
loss, wonder, and, 84–85; Morgan's *The American Beaver and His Works*, 108–10; pampas beavers on estancias, 82–84; performance, undisciplined research, and, 116–19; searching for, 113–16; sensoriums, 122–23; skin trade, empire, and, 67–69; traces, in Tierra del Fuego, 113–14, 113*f*; wonder and, 108
Beban, Fortunato, 151n38
Bec, Louis, 148n22
Benjamin, Walter, 128, 153n11
Berger, John, 12
Beschel, Roland, 59
Bessire, Lucas, 147n12
Boal, Augusto, 165n7
Braun, Mauricio, 98, 164n25
Bridges, E. Lucas, 3, 16, 38–40, 76, 98–99, 101, 101*f*, 151n36, 159n33, 164n29
Bridges, Thomas, 40, 76, 78, 84, 106
Briggs, Ellis, 97*f*
Button, Jemmy, 28, 35–39

Calderón, Cristina, 54, 55*f*, 138
Caleta Josephina estancia, 60*f*
La Candelaría mission, 163n22
canning factory, Rio Grande Estancia, 101
Cape Horn, 1*f*, 2, 8, 32*f*
capitalism, extractive, 75, 154n14
caracara, 81–82
carbon markets, 74
Carini, Peter, 138
Carruthers, David, 158n25
Carson, Rachel, 135–36
Castorera (A Love Story) (film), 125–26, 125*f*
cattle, 84
Cerro de las Onas, 81–82
Chalshoat, 51*f*, 96*f*, 101, 101*f*
Chapman, Anne, 7, 28–31, 130*f*, 131–32
Chatwin, Bruce, 3
Chevalley, Denis, 35
Chile: environmental movement in, 158n25; neoliberal economic system in, 158n18; salmon farming in, 155n10
Chiloé, 82

Chorillo los Perros creek, 63, 64*f*
ciexaus, 33–34, 34*f*
Colloredo-Mansfeld, Rudi, 107*f*, 108
colonialism: archival earth and, 50; decolonization, 42–43, 54; environmental change and, 12, 41; Furlong's archival self and, 17–18; genocide and reforestation, 49; inscription practices and, 32–33, 151n31; "moves to innocence," 163n16; "mud men," 33; multispecies mobility and, 78; salvage anthropology, 131, 136–37, 162n5; sawmills and settler belonging, 70–71; settler colonialism, defined, 154n15; World's End as figure and, 99. *See also* apparatuses; empire and imperialism; entanglements; inscription practices
"command and control" approach, 85
condors, 115, 134–35, 155n7
contact zones, 12, 147n19, 162n5
Cook, Frederick, 98
Cooper, John M., 161n55
Corcoran, Derek, 65, 82, 114–16, 125–26
Crosby, Alfred, 76
Curtis, Edward S., 92
cylinder recordings, 24, 136–40

Darwin, Charles: *Allen Gardiner* Massacre and, 37; association with the archipelago, 28–29; on Cape Horn, 8; as figure, 30; Fuegian captives, description of, 28–31; Furlong Papers and, 37; HMS *Beagle*, 28–29; topography and species named after, 30–31, 150n27; wonder and, 7–8; Wulaia Cove and, 39–41
Davis, Heather, 49
decolonization, 42–43, 54
de la Cadena, Marisol, 151n43
Deleuze, Gilles, 128
dermatoglyphs, 22–28, 22*f*, 25*f*, 27*f*, 149n5
Derrida, Jacques, 16, 52–53, 128–29, 137, 148n1, 164n30
Despard, George Pakenham, 36–37, 39–40, 99
diasporas, animal, 66–67, 78, 83–84

Dillemuth, Stephan, 165n2
dogs, Fuegian, 51f, 52, 154n1
Dreamworlds of Beavers (Gast, Ogden, and Marambio), 111f, 112–13
dualphotography, 96–97, 99

earth, archival, 38–43, 47–50
Ellis, Erle C., 153n5
empire and imperialism: beaver skin trade and, 67–69; ecological imperialism, 76, 84; environmental change and, 11–12; extinction fears and imperialist nostalgia, 92–94. *See also* colonialism
Ensayos, 116–17, 125–26
entanglements: archive and, 12, 53; beaver fur trade and, 69; Darwin and, 30; Furlong and, 99; invasive species paradigm and, 66; loss and, 6–7; multispecies mobility, estancias, and, 78; sheep complex and, 81, 83; time, entangled, 50, 64, 132; wonder and, 85; Wulaia Cove and, 41. *See also* apparatuses
environmental change and imperialism, 11–12, 41
environmentalism: beavers viewed as threat by, 63–64; Carson's *Silent Spring*, 135–36; in Chile, 158n25; sheep and, 81; timber industry and, 73–74
Escobar, Arturo, 44f, 45–46
estancias: animal diasporas on, 78; Caleta Josephina, 60f; Harberton, 22, 38, 76, 98, 159n33; horse-dog-human collaboration on, 52; life today on, 78–84; Marel, 83f; Remolino, 76–78, 93f; Rio Chico, 80, 80f; Rio Grande, 101–3, 164n29; Sara, 102, 164n29; sheep complex and, 76–84; timber industry and, 70–71; Viamonte, 98, 101–2; Vrsalovic (Wulaia), 41
eugenics, 23
European Encounters with the Yamana People of Cape Horn, before and after Darwin (Chapman), 31

Fanon, Frantz, 17
Fell, Robert, 36–37
feminism, speculative, 131

figures, defined, 2–3
Filgueira, Francisco, 11
fingerprint analysis, 23
Finkelstein, Maura, 148n21
FitzRoy, Robert, 28–30
Florida Everglades, 2–3, 14, 26, 44–45, 65
Flusser, Vilém, 148n22
footprints. *See* dermatoglyphs
Forestal Russfin, 71
forests, Fuegian: about, 69–70; beaver costumes in, 122–23; beavers in, 64, 64f, 69–75, 85; carbon markets and, 74; environmentalism and Pampas vs., 81; inscription practices and, 75; Karukinka Nature Park, 63, 64f, 74–75, 115, 117; Omora Ethnobotanical Park, 119f, 120, 122–23, 135–36; sawmills and timber industry, 70–74, 72f; Wildlife Conservation Society and, 74–75; wonder, loss, and, 134
fossils, trace, 24
Foster, Robert, 108
Foucault, Michel, 128, 154n14
foxes, gray, 78
Fraser, Crystal, 148n5
Frei, Eduardo, 158n25
Fuegian Archipelago: about, 2–3; Argentina's claims in the region, 106; Darwin, association with, 28–29; map, 1f; as real and imagined place, 7
Fugassa, Martín, 154n1
Furlong, Charles Wellington, 15f, 86f, 97f; archipelago description, 2; archival self, 16–20; articles by, 92–94, 99, 162nn2–3; on dogs, 51f, 52; as ethnographer, 86–90, 100; on forests and estancias, 69–70; Gusinde correspondence, 88–90; Isla Navarino map, 32f; journals, 18–20, 19f; Karukinka and, 63; "lone white man" subject position, 97–98; "Map of Tierra de Fuego," 161n55; on settlers, 98–99; Wulaia Cove, *Allen Gardiner* Massacre, and, 37–42. *See also specific topics, such as* photography
Furlong, Virginia Spinney, 15f

Furlong Papers, Dartmouth College: about, 11; Darwin's presence in, 37; establishment of, 87; origins, forgetting of, 53; photographs in, 92; proliferation of images from, 106; wax cylinder recordings in, 136–38; Yagán and Selk'nam communities and, 161n1
Fusco, Coco, 128

Galton, Francis, 23
Gardiner, Allen, 35
Garibaldi Honte, Luis, 131, 166n4
Gast, Christy, 59, 63, 67, 116–26, 138
genocide, 33, 49, 76, 94, 103, 131–32, 162n5, 166n6
Genskowski, Germán, 70–71
Ginzburg, Carlo, 150n10
Goldman Sachs, 74, 159n28
Gonzalez, Claudia, 33–34, 167n5
Goodall, Natalie, 159n33
Graells, Giorgia, 65–66, 114–16, 125–26
Gruber, Jacob, 162n5
guanacos, 10, 81, 147n17
Guattari, Félix, 128
Gusinde, Martin, 33–34, 88–90, 92–94, 106, 163n22

Hall, Stuart, 67
Handisyd, George, 61
handprints. *See* dermatoglyphs
Harald, King of Norway, 54, 55*f*
Haraway, Donna, 85, 131, 147n16, 160n51, 166n3
Harberton estancia, 22, 38, 76, 98, 159n33
Hartigan, John, 157n8
Hawley, Alex, 35
Herman, José, 106
Herschel, William, 23
Hill, Julia "Butterfly," 74
Hornbostel, Erich von, 137
hurricanes, 5
Hurston, Zora Neale, 145n5
hyper-anthropomorphism, 13

ibis, black-faced, 139
imperialism. *See* empire and imperialism

indigenous people: European representation of tropical and polar peoples, 146n7; historicized temporal categories and, 147n13; "lost tribes" trope, 9, 147n12; naming of, 2; nature associated with, 8–9; "vanishing race" motif, 92–94, 162n5. *See also* Selk'nam people; Yagán (Yaghan) people
inscription practices: beaver, 126; carbon markets as, 74; colonialism enacted through, 151n31; defined, 32–33; forests and, 75; gravestones, lichens, and, 60*f*; interpretive signs, 136; photography and, 96, 106; private inscription, 164n30; woodpecker drumming, 135
invasive species paradigm: animal diasporas vs., 66–67; beavers and, 64–69; biosciences research and, 156n4; "command and control" approach, 85; empire politics and, 68–69; killability and ethics of, 64–65
Ishtone, 96*f*
Isla Grande. *See* Tierra del Fuego
Isla Navarino, 42*f*; Furlong's map of, 32*f*; lichens, coastal, 57–61, 57*f*, 60*f*; Mejillones, 31–34; Museo Antropológico Martin Gusinde, 119–20; Omora Ethnobotanical Park, 119*f*, 120, 122–23, 135–36; schooling, 10; Wulaia Cove, 34–42, 41*f*

Karukinka Nature Park, 63, 64*f*, 74–75, 115, 117
Keyuk (Yanten Gomez), 132
Kiepja, Lola, 130*f*, 131–32
Klepeis, Peter, 79

Lacan, Jacques, 128
Lamb, Thomas, 68
Laris, Paul, 79
Larsen C, 5, 6
Laui, 77*f*, 78, 93*f*
lawn grass, 84
Lawrence, John, 31, 78, 93*f*
Lepselter, Susan, 150n19
Lévi-Strauss, Claude, 131
Lewis, Lily, 59

Lewis, Simon L., 49
Li, Tania Murray, 151n31
lichens, 10, 57–61, 57f, 60f, 147n16
Lidström, Susanna, 157n8
logging, 70–74, 72f
Loij, Angela, 130f
Lorimer, Jamie, 165n8
loss: about, 5–7, 134; biological species and, 84–85; forest loss and grief, 85; landscape of, 5; of language, 131–32, 136, 138, 140; photography and, 94; salvage anthropology and, 131, 136–37, 162n5; as subjective and political, 12; "vanishing race" motif, 92–94, 162n5
"lost tribes" trope, 9, 147n12
Lothrop, Samuel K., 161n55
Luciano, Dana, 153n9

MacLellan, Andrew "Red Pig," 102–3, 103f
Marambio, Camila, 59, 63, 114f, 116–26, 138, 165n2, 165n5
Marel estancia, 83f
Martínez, Ivette, 74
Martínez-Pasture, Guillermo, 64
Maslin, Mark A., 49
Maturana, Felipe, 94
Mavalwala, Janshed, 149n5
Mbembe, Achille, 154n16
Mejillones, 31–34
Memory, Boat, 28
Mendoza, Marcos, 8, 147n10
Minster, York, 28
Molina Vargas, Hema'ny, 167n11
Morgan, Lewis Henry, 108–10, 165n2
mud and mud worlds, 45–46
"mud men," 33
Museo Antropológico Martin Gusinde, 119–20

Najmishk, 100–101, 163n22
natural history museums, 53
nature: people associated with, 8–9; stability paradigm, 65–67; wonder and, 7–8, 134. *See also* Karukinka Nature Park

Nature Conservancy, the (TNC), 159n28
Navarino Island. *See* Isla Navarino

"Old Custan," 97f
Omora Ethnobotanical Park, 119f, 120, 122–23, 135–36, 167n5
Ondinnok, 130f
Orundelico, 151n33. *See also* Button, Jemmy
Otroshoal, 89f, 139
Overend, David, 165n8

pampas: history of, 76; sheep complex on, 76–84, 77f, 79f, 80f, 100–101, 101f
Paulson, Henry, 159n28
Peary, Robert, 98
performance: *Asunto Castor* (film and performance), 119–20, 120f, 124, 165nn6–7; *Beaver Dance* (film), 123–24, 124f; *Castorera (A Love Story)* (film), 125–26, 125f; thought experiments, 121, 126; undisciplined research and, 116–18; wonder and, 118
Petrigh, Romina, 154n1
Phillips, Garland, 37
photography: double exposures, 91f, 96; dualphotography, 96–97, 99; ethics of publishing, 96; Furlong's articles, 92–94; Furlong's Fuegian aesthetic, 94–96; Furlong's subject position, alone, 97–99; at Najmishk, 100–101; postcards and images for tourists, 92, 104–5, 105f; reproductive life of photographs, 104–6; running out of film and traveling for more, 102–3; state inscription and, 106; "vanishing race" motif, imperialist nostalgia, and, 92–94
Picton Island, 84
plastics in stratigraphic record, 49
Plumwood, Val, 157n6
Polanyi, Karl, 131
postcards, 104–5, 105f
Povinelli, Elizabeth, 154n14
Pratt, Mary Louise, 12, 147n19, 163n20
present, archives of: archive origins and forgetting, 52–53; assemblage of multiple temporalities, 50; earth archive,

present, archives of (*continued*) stratigraphic time, and, 48–50; evidence in, 12; Fuegian dogs, 51*f*, 52; natural history museums, 53; pantry for the apocalypse, 56; salmon farming and protest letter, 54–56; seed banks, 54; zoos, 53–54
Prieto, Alfredo, 11
Pringle, Anne, 58–59
puesteros (shepherds) and *puestos* (winter stations), 81–82. *See also* sheep and sheep herding
Punta Arenas, 98, 104–6
Puppup, 21*f*, 51*f*, 95, 96*f*, 101, 101*f*

rabbits, 78
racial stereotypes, 87
reforestation, 49
Remolino estancia, 76–78, 93*f*
rhea, lesser (Darwin's), 133*f*, 134
Rich, Nathaniel, 5
Rio Chico estancia, 80, 80*f*
Rio Condor project (Trillium), 73–74
Rio Grande estancia, 101–3, 164n29
Roca, Julio Argentino, 76
Root, Elihu, 98
Rosaldo, Renato, 92
Rozzi, Ricardo, 135

Saavedra, Barbara, 75
salmon farming, 54–56, 155n10
salvage anthropology, 131, 136–37, 162n5
Sara estancia, 102, 164n29
Savory, Allan, 81
sawmills, 70–71
Schwendener, Simon, 59
Selk'nam Corporation Chile, 167n11
Selk'nam language, 131–32
Selk'nam people: dermatoglyphs, 22–28; dogs, relationship with, 51*f*, 52; forced relocation of, 99, 132; Furlong's ethnographic information on, 87–90; *Hain* ceremony, 8, 9*f*; images of, 8–9; Najmishk village treated as ethnographic site, 100–101; name of, 2
Serrano, Alberto, 11, 54, 55*f*, 106

Serres, Michael, 153n10
sheep and sheep herding, 76–84, 77*f*, 79*f*, 80*f*, 98–101, 101*f*
Silent Spring (Carson), 135–36
Simpson, Audra, 165n2
social evolutionism, 23, 149n5
Sociedad Explotadora de Tierra del Fuego, 100–101
Solnit, Rebecca, 5, 10
Sonja, Queen of Norway, 54, 55*f*
South American Missionary Society, 35–39, 47*f*, 78
Spencer, Baldwin, 28
Srinivas, Tulasi, 146n6, 147n14
Stengers, Isabelle, 13, 148n26
Stewart, Kathleen, 28
Stirling, Waite H., 37
Stocking, George, 149n5
Stokes, Pringle, 30
Stoler, Ann Laura, 147n20
stratigraphic time, 48–51, 152n5, 153n12, 154n14
Subramaniam, Banu, 81
Syre, David, 73–74

TallBear, Kim, 154n14
Taussig, Michael, 19–20, 33, 166n2
thought experiments, 13, 121, 126
Thurman, Judith, 132
Tierra del Fuego: defined, 2, 145n3; ecological zones of, 79; Furlong's "Map of Tierra de Fuego," 161n55; Lago Fagnano, 138–39; map, 1*f*; sheep on, 79
timber industry, 70–74, 72*f*
time and temporalities: entangled time, 50, 64, 132; photography and, 106; stratigraphic time, 48–51, 152n5, 153n12. *See also* present
Tininisk, 139–40
Todd, Zoe, 49, 148n5
tourism and photography, 92, 104–5, 105*f*
trace evidence: archival earth, Anthropocene, and stratigraphic time, 48–51; dermatoglyphs, 22–28, 22*f*, 25*f*, 27*f*, 149n5; the Derridean trace, 129, 137–38; fossils, 24; Wulaia, 34–42, 41*f*

Trillium Corporation, 72f, 73–74
tropics as moral category, 146n7
Tsing, Anna, 6, 84–85, 147n15, 152n1
Tuck, Eve, 163n16

undisciplined research, 116–18
Ushuaia, 47f, 48, 106, 113
Uttermost Part of the Earth (Bridges), 3

Valle Hermoso, 113
van Dooren, Thom, 6
"vanishing race" motif, 92–94, 162n5. *See also* "lost tribes" trope
Veiga, Cándido, 104–5
Viamonte estancia, 98, 101–2
violence, colonial: *Allen Gardiner* Massacre, 35–40; genocide, 33, 49, 76, 94, 103, 131–32, 162n5, 166n6; "mud men" and, 33; sheep complex and shelter from, 76; stratigraphic time and, 50, 154n14; territorial edges of, 100
Vrsalovic, Antonio, 41, 151n41

Warkeeo, 22f, 89f, 139
Waters, Colin N., 153n5
wax cylinder recordings, 24, 136–40
West, Paige, 146n7, 167n5
Whitehouse, Andrew, 167n4
Whyte, Kyle, 147n13
Wildlife Conservation Society (WCS), 74–75, 117, 159n29
Wolf, Eric R., 67–68
Wolfe, Patrick, 50, 76, 154n15

wonder: about, 7–10, 134; cylinder recordings and, 138–39; hope and, 9–10; performance and, 118; species wonder, 84–85; speculative, 12–13; as subjective and political, 12
woodpecker, Magellanic, 135–36
World's End: European representation and, 146n7; as figure, 2–3, 99; photography and, 105–6; salmon farming protest and, 55–56; wild people and wild nature collapsed in, 8–9
World That Comes to an End—Lola, A (performance), 130f
Wulaia Cove, 34–42, 41f

Yagán language, 136, 138–39
Yagán (Yaghan) people: cylinder recordings and songs of, 24, 138–40; dermatoglyphs, 22–28; domed dwellings, 36f, 39f; Furlong's ethnographic information on, 87–90; images of, 8–9; name of, 2; Omora and, 136, 167n5; relationship with, 11; salmon farming protest and letter, 54–56, 55f; sheep herding, 76–78, 77f; Wulaia Cove and *Allen Gardiner* Massacre, 34–42
Yang, Wayne, 163n16
Yoyo, 100
Yusoff, Kathryn, 154n14

Zand, Tristan, 97, 99
zoos, 53–54